The Renewal
of Meaning
in Education

Responses to the
Cultural and Ecological Crisis
of Our Times

Cataloging-in-Publication Data
Renewal of meaning in education : responses to the cultural
and ecological crisis of our times / edited by Ron Miller.
  p. cm.
  ISBN 0-962-72323-1
  1. Miller, Ron   2. Education – Humanistic   3. Human
ecology — Study and teaching   4. Environment and children
  LC1011.R45 1993

The Renewal of Meaning in Education

Table of Contents

Foreword

Douglas Sloan

For nearly the last decade Ron Miller has provided indispensable leadership to all persons concerned to develop a truly holistic education. In his books and as founder and editor of the *Holistic Education Review*, he has made known and helped shape some of the most important aspects of the holistic education movement. Now in this book, and with the authors he has mustered for it, Ron Miller takes us another step on the way to making a holistic education a reality for our schools and children.

In his introduction, Miller points to the educational significance of the present crisis in human affairs. This crisis includes at once the continuing destruction of the environment and the loss of the life and beauty of nature; the virulence of spreading racism and narrow nationalisms; the indiscriminate extension into every sphere of life of what Erwin Chargaff has called "the devil's doctrine" in our science and technology — the view that "what we can do, we must do"; the unrelieved and worldwide destruction of cultural richness and sources of meaning as traditional cultures continue to collapse under the impact of the homogenizing influences of the modern mindset and its attendant institutions; a modern educational system that would force the children at an ever-earlier age into an adult culture already shot through with futility, greed, and banality. The dimensions of the crisis are many — and here the reality of holism confronts us with a dark vengeance, for each of the dimensions is interwoven with the others, and all demand to be grasped together as symptoms of a deeper crisis of the whole human being.

Such a crisis is a crisis for education and for educators on at least two counts. In the first place, our ways of knowing and our dominant conceptions of knowable reality — central concerns of education by its nature — are implicated in the crisis at every point. Reductionist and fragmenting ways of knowing, truncated conceptions and, hence, impoverished experiences of reality, the failure to nourish and, therefore, the atrophy of qualitative sensitivities in art, in state-craft, and in science, all bespeak a momentous educational failure.

The crisis is educational, furthermore, simply because it puts the children and the future of their earth at stake.

In this book Ron Miller has brought together a group of authors who share a three-fold concern. They are all aware of the importance of uncovering and rooting out the taken-for-granted assumptions of modern culture and education that lie at the heart of the crisis, and that continue to lead us ever deeper into it. These assumptions are predominantly those of a mechanistic, non-participative, instrumentalist, and sense-bound view of the world, including the world of human possibility. An exclusive reliance on them makes it almost impossible by definition for human beings to deal adequately with the intrinsically meaningful, the qualitatively rich and real, and the living. These dominant assumptions of the modern mind about reality also underpin the major dualisms of our culture — the splits between soul and body, quantity and quality, knowledge and values, history and nature; they undergird our major institutions and are further reinforced by these institutions; and their inculcation in the children is more often than not a major purpose of modern education. Several of the authors here provide important resources for calling to consciousness and breaking the destructive hold of these narrow assumptions about the world and our knowledge of it.

In the second place, all of the authors are concerned, positively, to develop holistic conceptions of reality and of education that can nourish human wholeness and meaning at their deepest sources, conceptions of reality that demand a whole new vision and restructuring of our education.

Finally, all of the authors are intent on addressing problems and shortcomings within current expressions of holistic education itself that must be dealt with if the movement is to achieve its own best goals. There are at least four such challenges facing the holistic education movement today.

One such challenge is the temptation to mix together every newly discovered source of human meaning hitherto neglected by the dominant forms of modern education, and to call the resulting potpourri the "holistic alternative." A main strength of the holistic education movement, to be sure, has been its recognition of sources of meaning and reality largely ignored, if not militantly denied, by mainstream modern education — sources such as "the new science," primordial and esoteric wisdom traditions, humanistic psychology, contemplative and prophetic religion, aesthetic experience, and others. To throw all of these indiscriminately into the same mix, however, tends to create a kind of educational-spiritual slush that can only obscure the clarity which the holistic education movement now most urgently needs.

This blending of everything into one mass tends to create a generalized concept of the spiritual that can speak, for example, of the educational importance of reverence and wonder, but that can never move to draw from these generalities more than the bare minimum of concrete guidance for the actual tasks of education. There is a tendency then for the spiritual to remain merely at an attitudinal level. The necessity is never taken up to develop spiritual insight with a rigor and specificity that can have real and detailed implications for the curriculum, for pedagogy, for our understanding of child development, and for our grasp of the social-communal tasks of education. And the major modern dualism between a narrow knowledge on the one side and a generalized spirituality of values and attitudes on the other is thereby perpetuated.

A second challenge to the holistic education movement is the extent to which it, like every other new movement in our time, is vulnerable to infection by the very assumptions of modern education it would seek to overcome. After all, the dominant materialistic, reductionist, and mechanistic assumptions of our culture are ones in which we have all been reared and educated. They are lodged in our marrow, and they serve in actuality to give us large components of the main world of our everyday experience. Exorcising them is no simple matter of deciding now to accept other assumptions. Even after we have become critically aware of them, these dominant assumptions of the modern mindset continue to work in us, and, just as we had thought we were rid of them, they return in unsuspected ways, for they form our deepest collective unconscious (much deeper and tenacious than the Jungian version). Mechanistic, sense-bound, reductionist assumptions about the world and how we come to know the world can continue to undercut and subvert the best intentions of holistic education itself.

To discover, for example, that meditative and contemplative practices can lead to the experience of new dimensions of reality does not mean that they should be introduced without the greatest of care into the education of children (or even of modern adults). Most meditative practices acquire their meanings as disciplines within certain spiritual contexts and for certain spiritual purposes. Since these practices often have a power unsuspected by the modern mind, to extract them from their original context without further ado not only risks denaturing and dragging them down, it can in many cases be a thoughtless playing with fire — especially if given to children and young people — despite and sometimes because of the therapeutic and calming effects these practices can initially produce. And to suppose that we can take over philosophical and meditative practices from traditional cultures simply to serve our own self-development purposes can be a form of cultural strip-mining no less instrumental and greedy than the exploitation of natural resources to satisfy our untransformed consumer desires.

Or, to push this example somewhat further, one hallmark of modern education already noted is its drive to impose adult modes of conceptuality and instrumental rationalism on young children at an ever-earlier age, oblivious of the real needs of the children and of the true foundations in play, imitation, and imagination of powerful and mobile adult conceptual abilities themselves. It will only be another variation on this modern propensity if holistic educators now impose on children, instead of practices in instrumental rationalism, procedures of meditation and visualization that may be appropriate for adults (which even with them require the utmost in discrimination and care) but that are perhaps entirely inappropriate and even dangerous for children.

These are instances of a good deal of the sorting out that the holistic education movement has yet to do. A contribution of this book is that most of the authors recognize the importance of this work of discrimination and have begun to provide help in undertaking it.

A third challenge facing holistic education is a standing temptation to turn completely inward and to avoid the hard tasks of social transformation that genuine inner transformation demands and can help make possible. The recalcitrance of institutions to change, and the subtle undetected workings, noted above, of our habitual assumptions about reality, can make us prone to remaining satisfied with a surface change in mood and feeling, without undertaking deeper social transformation. The authors in this book are keenly aware of this danger, and begin to address it.

A final challenge facing the holistic education movement is to realize that this personal and social transformation must go hand in hand with a fundamental cognitive transformation. Each mutually involves the others. We cannot, for instance, transcend the boundary experiences to which we are being brought by the as yet un-understood data of the new physics by attempting to grasp these data out of our old paradigms and ordinary capacities of perception and understanding. Nothing less than new cognitive faculties are required. Similarly, we cannot simply assimilate the ancient, newly rediscovered primordial wisdom to our untransformed, ordinary sense-bound modern consciousness. New capacities of insight and imagination must be developed. Nor, finally, can we begin to establish radically new political, economical, and ecological relationships apart from genuine new knowledge of the living forces and qualities in nature and of the wholeness of the human being, body, soul, and spirit. The basically nineteenth-century images and categories for understanding the human being, society, and nature that tend to be shared alike by our current liberals and conservatives, revolutionaries and reactionaries, whatever their other differences, will no longer suffice. In every case, the development of new cognitive capacities, new transformations of thinking, feeling, and willing as organs of perception and understanding are essential. This cognitive transformation will be central to an education of the whole person.

Actually beginning to develop this kind of education, with all its detailed implications for pedagogy, curriculum, educational governance, political, economic, and ecological relationships and practices, is what a genuine holistic education movement must be about. It is a task still in its earliest and most fragile stages. It is one which, as this book illustrates, is not without important resources and models, some actually of long standing. "The holistic education movement," writes Miller in his introduction, "is still working out its theoretical foundations." The working out of these foundations is crucial to all else. This book helps us understand better what this must involve.

Introduction

Vital Voices of
Educational Dissent

Ron Miller

The closing years of the twentieth century are posing severe challenges to conventional understandings of education. We are the first generation in the history of humanity to possess the power to annihilate most of the living species on Earth, including our own. We are the first generation to face the imminent decline of the ecological balance of the entire planet — a decline that our own technological wizardry and ecological ignorance have brought about. Nuclear power and weapons of mass destruction, artificial intelligence, biotechnology, and other advances in knowledge call for moral diligence on a scale unknown to previous generations, if we are to preserve the dignity and integrity of life. For centuries education was a quest to know, to progressively add to our knowledge — but now we are confronted by the realization that we know far more than we understand; we know too much, or more accurately, as Parker Palmer has observed, we know in ways that are violent and destructive, rather than in ways that enhance and nourish life (Palmer, 1983).

The knowledge explosion of our century also poses challenges of a more positive nature. The advance of communications technology puts us in instant contact with people around the world: Ideas are transferred across borders that previously resisted them (apparently the recent revolutions in eastern Europe were aided by fax machines). Cultural cross-fertilization — for example, the meeting of western and eastern religions — has broken down ancient boundaries to our self-knowledge. Research in neurophysiology, psychology and human science has given us a dramatically larger view of the capacities of the human mind. Post-Newtonian science and postmodern philosophy expose the narrowness of the modern world's picture of "reality" and provide a more dynamic, colorful, vibrant sense of life: Atoms dance and people create history — so we may now free ourselves from the dead hand of determinism and reductionism.

Given these rapidly unfolding developments in all areas of life, this is a time of uncertainty and transition in modern culture. The birth of a global economy is bringing about painful realignments of power and cultural identity. Racial hatred and ethnic rivalries spawn increasing violence in America, Europe, and elsewhere. Families and institutions collapse under the pressures and uncertainties of shifting values. Violent crime, corporate and political corruption, and addiction to drugs and entertainment siphon off our creative energy. Mass media bombard our senses, our consciousness, and subliminal awareness with persistent messages of violence, hedonism, and moral confusion. In response, religious and political fundamentalism offer a sense of security and stability and attract the allegiance of millions.

Surely an education designed for nineteenth century industrial society does not address the needs of our time. Our schools do not speak to the confused, fearful condition of the young generation who must inherit this troubled culture and this threatened planet. Consequently, American education has entered a period of upheaval and conflict from which it cannot emerge unchanged. Corporate leaders call for "excellence" and accountability, while mainstream politicians seek to educate for a globally competitive economic system; teachers demand greater professional autonomy, and minority communities and progressives work to make education responsive to a diverse multicultural society. Religious conservatives desert the public schools for more disciplined Christian academies and homeschooling, while more child-centered parents and educators seek greater freedom and meaningful learning for young people, sometimes through homeschooling as well. Some factions advocate greater choice, through vouchers or magnet schools, while others warn against abandoning the vision of common schooling. This last group will ultimately be the most disappointed, for the conflicts over education today result from the bare fact that there is no longer a societal consensus supporting the nineteenth century model of common schooling. A radically different paradigm, not yet clearly defined, is emerging.

The aim of this book is to build upon a premise that David Purpel articulated a few years ago in *The Moral & Spiritual Crisis in Education*: In the face of massive cultural upheaval, in the face of this breakdown of societal consensus, it is petty and small-minded for educators to concern themselves only with technical and managerial problems. Education today needs a new vision, a new understanding of its fundamental purposes. In order to move out of the crisis we are in, it is not enough to "restructure" the system already in place; educators must radically examine their underlying assumptions and convictions about the nature and purpose of schooling, for these are stale remnants of a simpler time. Therefore, rather than *restructure* our schools — that is, to try yet again to design a better institutional form for established assumptions — we need now to *deconstruct* the socially/culturally produced meanings of "education," "school," and "teaching." We need to examine the limitations of our nineteenth century conceptions and explore the possibilities of new meanings that can guide us — and more importantly, our children — into the twenty-first century.

The authors in this book are educators who have begun this task. I invited this particular group of authors because, among the scholars with whom I have had personal contact over the years, I felt they represented a good cross-section of those who are asking the most important questions in education today. I consider these scholars to be *holistic* in their orientation; that is, they represent an emerging paradigm in educational thinking that emphasizes wholeness and integration in the learning process, a nourishing and democratic community both inside the school and without, a global and ecological perspective on social and economic problems, and a recognition of the spiritual dimension of human existence (R. Miller, 1992; J. Miller, 1988; Lemkow, 1990). The holistic education movement is still working out its theoretical foundations, and it is a major purpose of this book to contribute to that effort. David Purpel and Kathleen Kesson explicitly address this need in their essays, but all the chapters that follow contribute to the emerging holistic critique of contemporary education.

Obviously, there are many other fine scholars raising these and additional questions, and some of their works are listed in the appendix at the end of this book. But I am indebted to my seven colleagues who have contributed to this book — first for their clear thinking and moral vision, and second for giving the time and effort to make this volume possible.

This book raises severe questions, provocative questions, about the meaning of education in a post-industrial world. How many educators, for example, have stopped to consider "the dangers of education" as David W. Orr does in the opening chapter? Orr argues that schooling, as it has been conceived in modern industrial society, alienates us from the natural world and from our own true callings as individuals. Conventional education imparts a disconnected, amoral curriculum that enables us to become efficient technicians and ambitious careerists, but not wise human beings. Orr contrasts the well-schooled Albert Speer, a leading figure in the Third Reich, with the ecologist Aldo Leopold's sensitivity to the moral lessons of the natural world. A major difference between them is that Speer lost his sense of joy and wonder toward life's mysteries, while Leopold deliberately cultivated his.

An education that substitutes curriculum, time-on-task, and SAT scores for wonder, imagination, and joy is an education that kills the human spirit and permits us to desecrate the Earth. Education must no longer be conceived in economic and utilitarian terms. In a penetrating critique of the "restructuring" movement that has followed in the wake of *A Nation at Risk*, Orr asserts that "the important facts of our time have more to do with too much economic activity of the wrong kind than they do with too little." He reminds us that since the time of Descartes and Bacon, scientific knowing has been associated with power, not wisdom, and our civilization's raw and stupid exercise of power now threatens to annihilate life on the planet. This recognition supports Parker Palmer's contention about the violence inherent in our way of knowing.

C.A. Bowers probes further into the nature of Cartesian thinking in his essay on the ecological crisis. He describes a number of related assumptions ("myths"), inherent in our culture's way of knowing, that treat persons as isolated, completely autonomous individuals and divide humanity as a whole from the rest of the natural world. This mindset further assumes that change, when rationally directed, equals progress — i.e., what is rational must be beneficial. While granting the many social and economic achievements of modern culture, Bowers argues that this worldview is not adequate to address the needs of the present historical moment. The ecological crisis demands that we overcome our atomistic individualism and recognize the cultural assumptions behind our ecologically destructive social, economic, and technological practices. We must then consciously choose new practices that are *sustainable* over the long run.

Drawing on Gregory Bateson's thinking, Bowers seeks to replace the Cartesian dualism of human and nature, mind and body, knower and known with a recognition of the "ecology" — that is, the holistic context — of any given human situation. "The individual is always part of a larger set of interactive relationships." It is only when we grasp this truth (and Bowers points out that it is difficult for people steeped in Cartesian thinking to fully grasp it) that we clearly see the need for a drastic transformation of society, technology, and education. Rational, incremental changes cannot heal the "interactive relationships" we have ruptured through our anthropocentric, mechanistic values and actions. Bowers calls for the educational process to embrace an ecological understanding of human existence. Not only should the curriculum enable students to question assumptions about science, progress, and humanity's use of "resources" — but the educator needs to become sensitively attuned to the ecology of the learning environment itself, which means becoming conscious of how language, textbooks and other materials, and other culturally defined elements actually create the context for individual learning. If education is "the introduction of youth into the patterns of the culture," then we must become responsible for the patterns we perpetrate.

The use of pat instructional techniques, the reduction of educational goals to behavioral outcomes and improved test scores, and the competitive individualism that pervades modern schooling all reflect the deep influence of Cartesian thinking. But we can no longer afford to turn out educators who are merely teaching technicians; if we are to restore a healthy "interactive relationship" between humanity and nature, then educators must be capable of facilitating such healthy relationships within the learning environment, between the students and the culturally charged language through which we introduce them to the values and belief system of the adult generation.

In the next essay, Jack Miller continues Orr's and Bowers's critique of the Cartesian/Baconian worldview. Miller, too, questions this atomistic, reductionistic, and fragmenting view that analyzes reality into segments ("atomic facts") which are presumed to interact mechanically, with no intrinsic relatedness. He observes that in this culture, the realms of art, beauty, creativity, ethics, and spirituality are clearly subservient to science, logic, technique, measurement and control. Our understanding of human development becomes narrowly behavioristic, the economic system is competitive and individualistic — "a social free-for-all" — and education inevitably follows a *transmission* model, in which a curriculum comprised of accepted facts is handed down to young people, who are assessed and vocationally sorted according to their ability to digest it. In the United States today, public policy takes for granted that this model is what "education" simply *is* — but Miller contrasts this dominant economic/utilitarian conception of education with alternative paradigms — the orientations of *transaction* and *transformation*.

The *transaction* model treats the learner as a capable decision maker and attempts to create a learning community that is responsive to students' interests, as in Deweyan progressive education. It is grounded in a liberal, pragmatist (and, I would add, classical Jeffersonian) philosophy that sees social institutions as amenable to reform and change, guided by a rational vision of human welfare. Many sincere educational reformers and researchers are moved by this vision. Still, its underlying conception of reality, as Miller observes, is scientific empiricism, an epistemology that leaves little room for "imagination, intuition, and most importantly a sense of the sacred." The transaction position is humanistic but not holistic.[1]

A holistic conception of education requires a model of *transformation*. Essentially, this involves the healing of the subject/object dualism that lies at the heart of the Cartesian worldview. "In the transformation position," says Miller, "the universe is seen as an interconnected whole." In his groundbreaking study *The Holistic Curriculum* (1988), Miller emphasized that holistic education is concerned with connections between linear thinking and intuition, mind and body, subject and knowledge, self and community, and between the individual's limited ego/persona and the "higher self." Holism sees these connections as intrinsic and organic, needing to be gently cultivated rather than technocratically managed. Holistic education returns us to the Latin root meaning of the word "education" — to *lead forth* what is naturally within the human being.

In his essay here, Miller asserts that holistic education is rooted in metaphor (as opposed to technique); this enables it to change and evolve in response to the existential and cultural situation of teacher and learner. In my view, this is a deeply important observation; when "holistic" education is defined according to specific methods, it is reduced to a caricature. We must not approach holistic education (or the "transformation" model, or whatever term we would apply to the kind of education described in this book) with the same assumptions that underlie conventional schooling. Here is where our project of deconstruction rather than restructuring is vital: We must see the teaching and learning process afresh, with new eyes and new hearts. Miller — along with many others in the holistic education movement — suggests that educators would do well to incorporate meditative practices into their work in order to genuinely achieve this fresh perception.[2]

Nevertheless, it is important to maintain a healthy *balance* between different modes of knowledge. Many advocates of holism, in their enthusiasm to promote intuitive, spiritual means of understanding, have largely abandoned the interpretive, critical tool of serious intellectual discourse. In recent writings, David Purpel (Purpel & Miller, 1991; Purpel, 1992) has called on the holistic education movement to embrace a more balanced perspective, and that is a main purpose of his essay here. Purpel reminds us that "there can be no educational policy or practice independent of a social and cultural context...." In one sense this statement supports C.A. Bowers in his view that the educational process is permeated with cultural meaning and can never be a narrowly technical or managerial project. Yet in all his writings Purpel is explicitly concerned as well with social, political, and economic injustice and takes educators to task for failing to confront it. Purpel's abhorrence of "unnecessary human suffering" defines his conception of education "in a prophetic voice," which is "an educational process directed at creating a just society and a compassionate culture."

A single-minded concern for inward, spiritual development neglects the social and cultural elements of this process. But an exclusively critical position is in danger of sinking into moral relativism and becoming overly cynical. Purpel finds a balanced social critique/spiritual vision in the world's religious traditions. He sees Socrates as an exemplary figure — one whose incisive, inquiring, skeptical mind served a genuine spiritual journey — and then shows how modern Western cultures may draw moral courage from the prophetic tradition described in the Bible. Yet there is no all-purpose moral solution to humanity's ills, he cautions: In every culture, in every historical moment, we are responsible for choosing a moral path that is "most resonant with our vision of a just, peaceful and joyous world." It is not clear how we are to ultimately evaluate the worth of our vision; this is where the complex dialectic between rational inquiry and interior revelation must be cultivated and practiced over the course of each person's lifetime.

Once again, the message for educators is that technique, curriculum, and quantifiable achievement cannot adequately draw forth (that is, educate) the moral consciousness that is demanded by today's culture-in-crisis. "The people cry out for meaning, wisdom and deliverance — and the society and school respond fearfully with more control, more jargon, more retrenchment, and less meaning and wisdom than ever." Purpel argues that so-called professionalism among educators serves to isolate education ever further from the pressing problems and challenges of our time. At this point in his essay, his prose heats up to prophetic intensity, as he charges that mainstream educators have utterly failed to address the severe crises that threaten the lives of every citizen, and every student, in our society.

There are, Purpel says, "important and vital voices of educational dissent," but they do not appear to be having a noticeable effect on educational policy. Again Purpel emphasizes the need to integrate the social/critical elements of this dissent with the personal/spiritual; the crisis of our time involves "material horrors" such as famine, oppression, and war *as well as* "diseases of the spirit" such as moral numbness and alienation. A genuine holistic education movement, like the prophetic tradition, would address the relationship between these realms of experience. Purpel points to the work of three diverse theologians — the Jewish scholar Abraham Joshua Heschel, the radical Catholic theologian Matthew Fox, and African-American theologian Cornel West — as superb contemporary expressions of the prophetic tradition.

As the radical progressive educator George Counts proposed sixty years ago (Counts, 1932), Purpel encourages educators to be agents of social and cultural transformation; it is not that schools can, in themselves, change society, but that the essential work of a true educator involves considering and striving toward our highest moral vision. Through education we express our vision of the good society. Surely there is a more meaningful and inspiring vision than the technicist, reductionist, narrowly economic agenda offered by our political and corporate elites. Purpel's passionate critique points the way toward such a vision.

Kathleen Kesson's work also guides us toward this vision. Her thinking integrates diverse expressions of critique and hope, including critical theory (both classical and contemporary), feminism, ecological science, Oriental and Native American worldviews, and a deep theoretical and experiential understanding of spiritual practices. Dissident educators need to draw from this rich variety of sources if we are to free ourselves from the pervasive economic reductionism of the dominant culture. Although Kesson is solidly within the camp of holism, she is disturbed that "many holistic thinkers [are] peculiarly unreceptive to an in-depth analysis of issues pertinent to their vision of social transformation." As her essay makes clear, the absence of such analysis could well cause the holistic movement to serve cultural and political agendas completely antithetical to its desired goals. A primary flaw in popular holistic thinking is its idealist, subjectivist, solipsistic epistemology; rather than linking mind and world, subject and object in a larger ecology of meaning (the aim of a genuine holism), this subjectivist holism reduces concrete historical and cultural issues to phenomena of personal consciousness. This is an "archaic" metaphysical assumption, according to Kesson — a philosophical position that is completely uninformed by the sophisticated contributions of critical theory and other contemporary explorations of language and culture. Like Purpel (and myself), Kesson sees holism as a way of understanding the *dialectic* between personal, spiritual development and structural social change.

Kesson's main point is that critical theory — as in the work of Horkheimer, Adorno, and Marcuse — is a powerful ally of holism, seeking a very similar cultural transformation: "the emancipation of consciousness, the nurturing of a decentralized political movement, and the reconciliation of humanity and nature." The two approaches represent very different styles of thought: Holism embodies the raw energy of cultural transformation — the search for wholeness, meaning and authenticity expressed by Transcendentalist romantics in the 1830s and by the explosion of movements for personal growth and social change in the 1960s. Critical theory is a far more sober response to the oppression and totalitarianism of the twentieth century. Yet to deal with the breakdown of industrial society as we enter the twenty-first century, we need both energy and sobriety, soaring vision and critical scrutiny, optimism and skepticism. Our culture is adrift, and these are dangerous times.

The utilitarian rationalism that undergirds modern consciousness is under attack, and the question is whether it will be replaced by an irrational exaltation of "nature" (as in Fascism), or a more advanced reason "capable of incorporating the nonrational, suppressed aspects of consciousness without sacrificing its critical capacity." Holism can lead to the former — it can be manipulated by reactionary cultural forces — unless its enthusiasm is tempered by careful, sober understanding of these cultural forces. Kesson emphasizes this point dramatically in her discussion of "spiritual technologies" (imagery exercises, subliminal programming, accelerated learning, and the like) and the ways in which these are already being used to reinforce, rather than transform, the cultural status quo. Because these technologies for the development of nonrational faculties are morally and culturally neutral, "they are not, in themselves, an adequate foundation upon which to build a comprehensive holistic education theory." (This is the point I made earlier about a holistic approach comprised only of particular methods being a "caricature.")

Kesson goes on to examine issues of inequality and stratification in education, and how holistic approaches might unwittingly exacerbate rather than address these problems. So long as the public school system fundamentally serves to categorize young people according to their vocational destinies (Miller, 1992, p. 42), any new approach or instructional technology will be harnessed to this sorting function. "Whole-brain" learning models, affective learning, and critical problem solving are not designed to prepare people to work on assembly lines but to hold professional and managerial positions. As the professional and managerial class receives an even richer and fuller education, the gap between them and the underclass — and the gap between developed and developing nations — grows ever wider.

Finally, Kesson reflects on the "sensitive role" that educators play in children's lives: "As mediators of cultural experience, they dwell in the nexus of the 'subjective' worlds of children and the 'objective' world of cultural experience." It is this nexus that makes education such a complex and difficult endeavor! Public schooling roughly imposes the "world of cultural experience" onto the inner worlds of children, but it is no less imbalanced to surrender entirely to subjectivity and spontaneity. As I put it in discussing the Summerhill/free school model, there are numerous social, psychological, moral, and spiritual questions involved in educating a growing human being, "and they are not sufficiently answered with an all-purpose prescription of 'freedom' or 'democracy'" (Miller, 1991, Fall, p. 30). John Dewey emphasized this point, and it is discussed in the interesting context of archetypal psychology by Australian scholar Bernie Neville (1989). Holistic education at its best is not merely a "child-centered" education; as Kesson argues, it is a thoughtful, critical, and radical effort to provide a nurturing cultural environment for the development of human capacities.

The final two essays of this series reflect the perspectives of two alternative educational paradigms — Waldorf education and the Whole Language movement. The scope of holistic education is much wider, of course, embracing progressive and humanistic approaches, open classrooms and "whole brain" methods, public and independent alternatives, Montessori education, cooperative learning, global education, and much more (Miller, 1991). The essays in this volume demonstrate how two of these approaches offer coherent and fully articulated theoretical alternatives to the industrial-age, Cartesian conception of schooling.

Waldorf education is built on a decidedly anti-Cartesian epistemological foundation. As Jeffrey Kane explains in the essay that follows, Rudolf Steiner, the founder of Waldorf pedagogy, held that ideas are a living reality — indeed, the fundamental reality that lies behind all apparent phenomena. Ideas live within the world as well as through the human mind and connect us intrinsically to the ongoing stream of existence. Kane argues that conventional schooling is inadequate because it treats knowledge as "passive and impersonal ... a possession rather than a generative aspect of intelligence ... decontextualized and static...." Knowledge is far more active, complex, and meaningful than mere information, and an education concerned only with information, facts, and so-called basic skills demeans the human quest to comprehend the fullness of experience.

As Kane shows in his reflection on the Copernican revolution, the human mind is capable of transcending apparent empirical "facts" and can penetrate to the "world of formative ideas." Through the power of imagination, we are able to *integrate* the empirical with the ideal, to place the concrete facts of our experience into a larger context of meaning, evolution, and purpose. Physicist David Bohm calls this context "undivided wholeness in flowing movement." Gregory Bateson called it "the pattern which connects." Spiritual traditions have called it the Absolute, the Tao, or God. It is the infinitely creative source of Being.

For Steiner, a living knowledge that connects us with this deeper source is knowledge that is experienced with one's entire being — the mind, the feelings, and the will. It is not enough to have ideas that "rest in the head as upon a couch"; they must activate energies within the soul. Kane observes that "experience of this sort is based upon encounter rather than control, respect rather than manipulation, understanding rather than utility." This is a succinct description of the differences between holistic education and conventional schooling. Holistic education, the Waldorf approach in particular, deals with "the interior landscapes of our own humanity"; from fairy tales for young children to the study of history by adolescents, this manner of education is more concerned with drawing forth the latent capacities and sensitivies of the soul than with stuffing passive young minds full of predigested information. It is an education that prepares young people to live purposefully, creatively, and morally in a complex world.

Kane recognizes that to modern thinkers, notions such as living ideas, interior landscapes, and sensitivities of the soul are largely foreign. Cartesian thinking finds it "difficult, if not impossible, to understand how the human qualities affect cognitive processes." Steiner, writing in the early years of the twentieth century, was far ahead of his time in envisioning a holistic, spiritually informed worldview that would eclipse the barren materialism of the scientific-industrial era. But the essays in this book reflect the possibility that Steiner's vision (though in many forms and terminologies) is being shared more and more widely.

In contrast to the Waldorf movement, the Whole Language approach is an emerging revolution within the public school system. In her essay, Lois Bridges Bird provides a concise introduction to the key tenets of Whole Language. It is a learner-centered pedagogy tracing its roots back to Comenius, Pestalozzi, and Dewey, yet its emergence as a coherent approach is based upon contemporary research in psychology, linguistics, and other social sciences. "In fact," Bird comments, "Whole Language establishes scientific credibility for the good intuitions progressive educators have always had about how human beings learn.... "

Although holistic education as a moral critique does not depend on "scientific credibility," Bird's essay again points to the integration of rational, empirical ways of knowing with the intuitive and imaginative — a recurring theme in this volume and an essential quality of holistic theory and practice. The point is this: "Whole

Language is not just a new scientific way to teach reading and language arts"; it is not a technique or methodology, blessed by the professional imprimatur of science, that educators can merely insert into a conventional learning environment. Rather, Whole Language is a vision of learner-oriented education "embedded within a socio-political context"; in other words, it is a holistic critique that draws from an integrated understanding of human development.

The field of sociopsycholinguistics does provide strong empirical support to this understanding. The work of Ken Goodman, Michael Halliday, Carole Edelsky, and others has demonstrated that language is a fluid, evolving tool which communities and persons use to establish meaning. This "scientific" fact has moral and political implications, as Paulo Freire and Lev Vygotsky have shown. When language and culture are seen as sacred repositories of truth, when so-called "cultural literacy" is put forward as the ruling purpose of education — then education merely serves to uphold the worldview and social institutions already in place, as well as the elites who benefit most from those institutions. But when we take hold of our cultural conditioning through a critical use of language (this is exactly the point C.A. Bowers makes in his work), we claim the power to reframe meaning and recreate society.

Whole Language theorists consistently emphasize that reductionist methods of language instruction — basal readers and skill-building workbooks, an exclusive reliance on phonics, etc. — tear meaning from the heart of literacy. "The complex, integrated processes involved in human language and learning suffer greatly when reduced to a piecemeal presentation," says Bird, who is especially critical of "education's alignment with behavioral psychology" for reducing the meaningful use of language into "the manipulation of abstract bits." Here we should recall Jack Miller's discussion of the theoretical roots of behaviorism in the Cartesian/Baconian worldview; the fact that Whole Language theorists have embraced an alternate model of scientific knowing — naturalistic inquiry, as practiced by many cultural anthropologists — is another important signal that Whole Language represents a radical break with the dominant educational paradigm.

Bird goes on to describe how the curriculum in a Whole Language environment is integrated; "the disciplines are not broken down into isolated skills and taught in separate segments of time, but rather are used to help students conduct real-life inquiry, to pursue questions that are of real interest to them." Once we are free of the "transmission" model of education (what Freire called the "banking" model, in which teachers deposit knowledge into passive student receptacles), students come to be viewed as active, inquisitive, meaning-seeking beings engaged in their own growth. Steiner, Montessori, and all insightful educators have asserted that this is in truth the essential nature of the human being. This is why it is so devastating, as David Orr reminds us, to replace the curiosity, wonder, and joy that characterize natural learning with the mechanical routines of conventional schooling. It is not sentimental and romantic to offer children a free and nurturing learning environment — it is essential to their development as whole human beings. Bird recognizes this in comparing Whole Language to literacy development within the family. This is also why thousands of families have abandoned the schools for home education (Holt, 1989; Gatto, 1992).

Again, Whole Language is not a classroom technique — it is a theory of natural learning. Bird offers several examples of experiential learning that involves students in meaningful ways in the ongoing life of the larger community. Eliot Wigginton's famous *Foxfire* project should not be seen as an isolated experiment in extracurricular activity, but as a superb model of the kind of education we ought to be providing to all young people. Wigginton himself has written that "we have rejected forever those teaching materials that have sucked all the life from our language arts classes and have destroyed our students' enthusiasm for the work.... We have passed a mile marker in our careers, and we will never return to materials and activities that anesthetize our students as surely as a surgeon's drugs. We will quit teaching first" (Wigginton, 1991). Strong stuff! It is hard to imagine an educator being so passionately attached to a new technique or instructional fad; clearly, we are dealing here with a sea change in education, a complete paradigm shift. There is revolution in the air.

Finally, Bird draws attention to the renewal of creativity and responsibility among Whole Language educators themselves. A teacher in a Whole Language environment needs to be a sensitive observer and interpreter of students' developmental processes. It is only out of this firsthand knowledge that educators can truly assess educational achievement or design learning activities relevant to students' lives. Furthermore Bird, like Purpel, asserts that educators need to address "the political nature of education" and claim their rightful role as moral activists in the political arena.

Here, then, are seven vital voices of educational dissent.

Although these voices reflect diverse perspectives and approaches, several common themes emerge, themes that define the holistic critique of contemporary education and culture. Before closing this introduction to the essays, I would like to briefly examine these themes and some of the issues they raise.

Themes of Holistic Education

In these writings there is a deep concern for **connection, relatedness, and integration in human experience**. The individual person is seen not as an isolated atom but as a nexus of intrinsic connections to social, cultural, biological, and spiritual environments. Human existence is woven into the fabric of the natural world in fabulously complex patterns, and all meaning ultimately derives from these patterns. Holistic educators hold that the knower is inherently involved in defining what is known; a genuine education enables the learner to make these definitions actively and conscientiously, developing a moral as well as intellectual framework for understanding the world. This orientation rejects Cartesian subject/object dualism and the fact/value dualism that plagues modern modes of knowing. Postmodern physics and biology, deep ecology, and nondualistic spiritual traditions all support this holistic, integrated epistemology. This is the foundation for the holistic critique of conventional schooling.

In these voices of educational dissent we find a **sense of reverence toward nature and life** that is very different from the modern project of analysis, quantification, and control. There is a respect for diversity, spontaneity, and the inherent wisdom of organic growth. There is a recognition that the most meaningful and noble aspects of human experience lie beyond the grasp of utilitarian reason and economic development.

The holistic perspective draws our attention to the profound relationship between spirituality, ecology, and social justice. Spirituality — a sense of reverence and awe in response to the mystery of life — leads us to appreciate the larger context — the ecology — within which our lives have meaning. Several of the authors in this volume, along with theologians like Heschel, Fox, and West, emphasize that we must extend this sense of reverence beyond the personal and subjective (including a subjective appreciation of nature) to involve the social and cultural sphere as well. A holistic perspective acknowledges that spiritual, planetary, and social ecologies *co-exist*, and describes the *multiple contexts of meaning* within which human existence is situated, from the raw physical and biological to the personal and psychological, to the social, cultural, planetary, and spiritual (Miller, 1991, Fall).

Holism, then, is the recognition that spiritual enlightenment, ecological awareness, and the quest for social justice must be brought together in order to adequately confront the crisis of our time. We need a reverence for life that finds expression in all contexts of human experience. (Matthew Fox's Creation Spirituality, which is at once thoroughly mystical, rooted in ecological thinking and postmodern science, and passionately concerned with social justice, is a particularly coherent and eloquent expression of the holistic critique of modern culture. See Fox, 1988, 1991).

Another theme that runs through many of these essays is the view that **people create meaning, and culture consequently evolves**. We interpret our experience through language and metaphor, and although cultures tend to reify these interpretations and render them static, it is possible to develop a critical consciousness that challenges the hegemony of the dominant culture. Purpel refers to this as the prophetic voice. The major purpose of schooling, as it has been conceived until now, has been to preserve the hegemony of the established culture — to induct each new generation into the dominant worldview. This is what Jack Miller calls the "transmission" model of education. But we can conceive education differently, as a genuine community of learning in which new meanings, new metaphors are generated. This requires a wholly different understanding of knowledge and learning — an ecological rather than dualistic understanding — and a radically different view of the social role of education. We must view education as a means of bringing forth new life, new meaning, new possibilities in each generation.

In times of cultural stability, when moral values bind together a human community and give satisfying meaning to individuals' lives, this radical conception of education is marginalized. Dissident educators have been dismissed as child-centered romantics through most of the past two centuries (Miller, 1992). We would argue that there is always a need for prophetic criticism and cultural evolution — the most stable societies may also be the most repressive, and life is continually evolving no matter how adequate a culture appears to be for a time. But radical dissent tends to be ignored until evolution leads to crisis. And in the late twentieth century, we have reached a crisis. With modern culture in upheaval, with accelerating social, personal and ecological disintegration, the need for new meanings, new metaphors and new values is becoming critical. These voices of educational dissent arise now in response to this crisis.

In order to generate new meanings, **it is essential that we draw upon our deepest source of renewal and creativity: the imagination.** In various ways, the educators in this volume emphasize the need for a way of knowing that goes beyond instrumental reason. David Orr speaks of the sense of wonder; Jack Miller points to the arts and meditation practice; Jeffrey Kane introduces us to Rudolf Steiner's understanding of "living knowledge" that is at once mystical and philosophically profound, transcending the centuries-old stalemate between empiricism and idealism; and Lois Bird describes "multiple meaning systems" and "alternative ways of creating and communicating" such as dance, art, and music.

None of these authors proposes that we simply reject reason or disciplined inquiry; rather, the holistic critique calls for an *integration* of rational, empirical, analytical modes of knowing with the imaginative and intuitive. As Kathleen Kesson suggests, we are at a point of cultural evolution that requires us to develop a more advanced reason, able to deal with the complex realities of our age. This is not the time to regress to the irrational. I would add that the work of Carl Jung is especially relevant to this issue; Jung reminds modern culture that the vast realm of the unconscious holds a significant portion of our psychic heritage and identity which can never be swept away by instrumental reason or technological progress. As our orderly, logical reason becomes more refined and more powerful, we must remain in touch with the primal forces of the unconscious through dreams and imagery, arts and meditation, intuition and imagination. This is the only way we can cultivate the "moral diligence" which, at the beginning of this essay, I indicated was our most crucial need. The humanist notion of a purely rational morality fails to account for the archetypal forces that rage through the psyche and history; Jung's call for the integration of reason and unconscious reflects, in a holistic sense, a more complete understanding of the human condition.

The difference between holistic and reductionistic paradigms comes down to this: Do we imagine an education that nourishes the creative, organic unfolding of life, one that holds reverence for the mysterious energies of our existence on Earth that Aldo Leopold (quoted in David Orr's essay) so poetically describes as a "fierce green fire"? Or is our imagination so blunted by Cartesian dualism and economic obsessions that the highest purpose we can envision for schooling is to make American corporations more competitive in the world marketplace? The first vision stirs the human soul and engenders the highest and noblest possibilities of our species. The other vision degrades us. Now, after three centuries of mechanistic science and a century and half of mechanistic education, we have an opportunity to choose the more inspiring vision.

References

Counts, G. (1932). *Dare the school build a new social order?* New York: John Day.

Fox, M. (1988). *The coming of the cosmic Christ.* San Francisco: Harper & Row.

Fox, M. (1991). *Creation spirituality: Liberating gifts for the peoples of the earth.* San Francisco: Harper & Row.

Gatto, J. T. (1992). *Dumbing us down: The hidden curriculum of compulsory schooling.* Philadelphia: New Society Publishers.

Holt, J. (1989). *Learning all the time.* Reading, MA: Addison-Wesley.

Lemkow, A. F. (1990). *The wholeness principle: Dynamics of unity within science, religion and society.* Wheaton, IL: Quest Books.

Miller, J. P. (1988). *The holistic curriculum.* Toronto: Ontario Institute for Studies in Education Press.

Miller, R. (1992). *What are schools for? Holistic education in American culture,* 2nd Ed. Brandon, VT: Holistic Education Press.

Miller, R. (Ed.). (1991). *New directions in education: Selections from Holistic Education Review.* Brandon, VT: Holistic Education Press.

Miller, R. (1991, Fall). Holism and meaning: Foundations for a coherent holistic theory. *Holistic Education Review* 4(3), 23–32.

Neville, B. (1989). *Educating psyche: Emotion, imagination and the unconscious in learning.* Blackburn, Australia: Collins Dove.

Palmer, Parker J. (1983). *To know as we are known: A spirituality of education.* San Francisco: Harper & Row.

Purpel, D. E., & Miller, R. (1991, Summer). How whole is holistic education? *Holistic Education Review* 4(2), 33–36.

Purpel, D. E. (1992, Spring). Bridges across muddy waters: A heuristic approach to consensus. *Holistic Education Review* 5(1), 17–26.

Wigginton, E. (1991). Get the radio man! In Kenneth S. Goodman, Lois Bridges Bird, & Yetta M. Goodman, (Eds.), *The Whole Language Catalog.* Santa Rosa, CA: American School Publishers, p. 220.

Notes

1. The difference between humanistic (rational, empirical) and holistic (ecological, spiritual) paradigms was made evident at a major symposium on educational restructuring held in 1987 and published in 1989 as *Schooling for tomorrow: Directing reforms to issues that count* (Needham Heights, MA: Allyn & Bacon). Twenty respected scholars—nearly all of them liberal, progressive, and deeply concerned with the shortcomings of conventional schooling—described an educational model rooted in a narrow scientific/technological worldview. I reviewed this book in *Holistic Education Review* 4(2) (Summer, 1991) and pointed out six fundamental assumptions implicitly shared (never explicitly acknowledged) by these researchers. Their key assumption is that "the only valid knowledge is empirical, analytical, intellectual, and utilitarian." I concluded that the book did *not* describe "schooling for tomorrow" nor did it ever address the issues that count most; instead, it puts forth a conception of education rooted in nineteenth century epistemology, not the ecological, social, economic, and existential challenges that we will face in the twenty-first century.

2. David W. Brown makes this point in "Possessing a Beginner's Mind: The Missing Link to Restructuring," *Holistic Education Review* 4(4) (Winter, 1991), pp. 21–24. He borrows the concept of "beginner's mind" from Zen meditation practice, specifically from Suzuki. "It is a mind that is open, and it includes both an attitude of doubt and possibility, as well as the ability to see things always fresh and new." A new teacher education program at the Naropa Institute, a Buddhist-oriented college in Boulder, Colorado, places meditative practice at the heart of the training. Their rationale is explained in Richard C. Brown, "Buddhist-Inspired Early Childhood Education at the Naropa Institute," *Holistic Education Review* 4(4) (Winter, 1991), 16–20.

Chapter 1

The Dangers of Education

David W. Orr

We are now preparing to launch yet another of our periodic national crusades to improve education. I am in favor of improving education, but what does it mean to improve education and what great ends will that improved education serve? The answer now offered from high places is that we must equip our youth to compete in the world economy. The great fear is that we will not be able to produce as many automobiles, VCRs, digital TVs, or supercomputers as the Japanese or Europeans. In contrast, I worry that we *will* compete all too effectively on an earth already seriously overstressed by the production of things economists count and too little production of things that are not easily countable such as well-loved children, good cities, forests, stable climate, healthy rural communities, sustainable family farms, and diversity of all sorts. The educational reforms now being proposed have little to do with the goals of personal wholeness, or the pursuit of truth and understanding, and even less to do with the great issues of how we might live within the limits of the earth. The reformers aim to produce people whose purposes and outlook are narrowly economic, not to educate citizens, and certainly not, as Aldo Leopold once proposed, "citizens of the biotic community."

The important facts of our time have more to do with too much economic activity of the wrong kind than they do with too little. Our means of livelihood are everywhere implicated in the sharp decline of the vital signs of the earth. Because of our fossil fuel-based economies and transportation systems we are now conducting a vast and risky experiment with global climate. The same systems have badly damaged the ozone layer. The way we produce food and fiber is responsible for the loss of 24 billion tons of soil each year, the sharp decline in biological diversity, and the spread of deserts worldwide. The blind pursuit of national security has left a legacy of debt, toxicity, and radioactivity that will threaten the health and well-being of those purportedly defended for a long time to come. And what Langdon Winner calls our "technological somnambulism" continues to issue forth a stream of technologies and systems of technology that do not fit the ecological dimensions of the earth.

Most of this was not done by the unschooled. Rather it is the work of people who, in Gary Snyder's words:

> make unimaginably large sums of money, people impeccably groomed, excellently educated at the best universities — male and female alike — eating fine foods and reading classy literature, while orchestrating the investment and legislation that ruin the world. (Snyder, 1990, p. 119)

Education, in other words, can be a dangerous thing. Accordingly, I intend to focus on the problem *of* education, not problems *in* education. It is time, I believe, for an educational *perestroika* by which I mean a general rethinking of the process and substance of education at all levels beginning with the admission that much of what has gone wrong with the world is the result of education that alienates us from life in the name of human domination, fragments instead of unifies, overemphasizes success and careers, separates feeling from intellect and the practical from the theoretical, and unleashes on the world minds ignorant of their own ignorance. As a result, an increasing percentage of the human intelligence must attempt to undo a large part of what mere intellectual cleverness has done carelessly and greedily.

Anticipations

Most ancient civilizations knew what we have forgotten: that knowledge is a fearful thing. To know the name of something is to hold power over it. Misused, that power would break the sacred order and wreak havoc. Ancient myths and legends are full of tales of people who believed that they were smarter than the gods and immune from divine punishment. But in whatever form, eating from the tree of knowledge meant banishment from one garden or another. In the modern world this Janus-like quality of knowledge has been forgotten. Descartes, for example, reached the conclusion that "the more I sought to inform myself, the more I realized how ignorant I was." Instead of taking this as a proper conclusion of a good education, Descartes thought ignorance was a solvable problem and set about to find certain truth through a process of radical skepticism. Francis Bacon went even further to propose an alliance between science and power which reached fruition in the Manhattan Project and the first atomic bomb.

There were warnings, however. Displaced tribal peoples commonly regarded Europeans as crazy. In 1744, for example, the Chiefs of the Six Nations declined an offer to send their sons to the College of William and Mary in these words:

> Several of our young people were formerly brought up at the colleges of the northern provinces; they were instructed in your sciences; but when they came back to us, they were bad runners, ignorant of every means of living in the woods ... neither fit [to be] hunters, warriors, nor counsellors, they were totally good for nothing. (McLuhan, 1971, p. 57)

Native Americans detected the lack of connectedness and rootedness that Europeans, with all of their advancements, could not see in themselves. European education incapacitated whites in ways visible only through eyes of people whose minds still participated in the creation and for whom the created order was still enchanted. In other words, European minds were not prepared for the encounter with wilderness nor were they prepared to understand those who could live in it. One had to step out of the dominant Eurocentrism and see things from the outside looking in. A century later Ralph Waldo Emerson was moving toward a similar conclusion:

> We are shut up in schools and college recitation rooms for ten or fifteen years, and come out at last with a bellyful of words and do not know a thing. We cannot use our hands, or our legs, or our eyes or our arms. We do not know an edible root in the woods. We cannot tell our course by the stars, nor the hour of the day by the sun. (Emerson, 1839; 1957, p. 136)

These and other warnings were forebodings of a much more serious problem that would gain momentum in the century to come. I think this becomes clearer in a comparison of two prominent but contrary figures of the middle years of the 20th century.

One, Albert Speer, was born in Germany in 1905 to a well-to-do upper middle class family. His father was one of the busiest architects in the booming industrial city of Mannheim. Speer attended a distinguished private school and later various Institutes of Technology in Karlsruhe, Munich, and Berlin. At the age of 23 Speer became a licensed architect. He is not known to us for his architecture, however, but for his organizational genius as Hitler's Minister of Armaments. In that role he kept World War II going far longer than it otherwise would have by keeping German arms production rising under the onslaught of Allied bombing until the final months. For his part in extending the war and for using slave labor to do so, Speer was condemned by the Nuremburg Tribunal to serve 20 years at Spandau prison.

I think his teachers and professors should share some of the blame for his actions. For example, in his memoirs Speer describes his education as apolitical:

> [It] impressed upon us that the distribution of power in society and the traditional authorities were part of the God-given order of things.... It never occurred to us to doubt the order of things. (Speer, 1970a, p. 8)

The result was a generation without defenses against the seductions of Hitler and the new technologies of political persuasion. The best educated nation in Europe had no civic education when it most needed it. Speer was not appreciably different from millions of others swept along by the current of Nazism.

The purge of June 30, 1934, was a moral turning point after which Speer silenced all doubts about his role in the Nazi hierarchy:

> I saw a large pool of dried blood on the floor. There on June 30 Herbert Von Bose, one of Papen's assistants, had been shot. I looked away and from then on avoided the room. But the incident did not affect me more deeply than that. (Speer, 1970a, p. 53)

Speer had found his Mephistopheles:

> After years of frustrated efforts I was wild to accomplish things — and twenty-eight years old. For the commission to do a great building, I would have sold my soul like Faust. Now I had found my Mephistopheles. He seemed no less engaging than Goethe's. (Speer, 1970a, p. 31)

In looking back over his life near its end, Speer said:

> My moral failure is not a matter of this item and that; it resides in my active association with the whole course of events. I had participated in a war which, as we of the intimate circle should never have doubted, was aimed at world dominion. What is more, by my abilities and my energies I had prolonged that war by many months.... Dazzled by the possibilities of technology, devoted crucial years of my life to serving it. But in the end my feelings about it are highly skeptical. (Speer, 1970a, pp. 523–524)

Finally in what certainly would be among the most plaintive lines penned by any leading figure of the twentieth century, Speer wrote:

the tears I shed are for myself as well as for my victims, for the man I could have been but was not, for a conscience I so easily destroyed. (Speer, 1970b, p. 96)

If Speer and the years between 1933–1945 seem remote from the issues of the late twentieth century, one has only to change the names to see the relationship. Instead of World War II, think of the war being waged against nature. Instead of the Holocaust think of the biological holocaust now underway in which perhaps 20% of the life forms on the planet in the year 1900 will have disappeared by the year 2000. Instead of the fanaticism of the 1000-year Reich, think of the fanaticism inherent in the belief that economies have no limits and can grow forever. Speer's upbringing and formal education provided neither the wherewithal to think about the big issues of his time nor the good sense to call these by their right names. I do not think for a moment that this kind of education ended in 1945 or that it was or is characteristic just of Europe. It is the predominant mode of education almost everywhere in an age of instrumental rationality that still regards economic growth as the highest goal.

Aldo Leopold was the son of a prosperous furniture manufacturer in Burlington, Iowa, and, like Speer, had all of the advantages of good upbringing. Leopold's lifelong study of nature began as a boy in the nearby marshes along the Mississippi River. His formal education at Lawrence Academy in New Jersey and Yale University were, I think, rather incidental to his self-education which consisted of long walks over the nearby countryside. Leopold was an outdoorsman who over a lifetime of rambling developed the ability to observe in nature what others only saw. He was a keen student of nature and it was this capacity that makes Leopold interesting and important to us. Leopold grew from a rather conventional resource manager employed by the U.S. Forest Service to become a scientist/philosopher who asked questions about the proper human role in nature that no one else bothered to ask. This progression led him to discard the idea of human dominance and propose more radical ideas based on our citizenship in the natural order.

Where Speer had seen human blood on the floor and turned away, Leopold described a different kind of turning point that took place on a rimrock overlooking a river in the Gila Wilderness in 1922. Leopold and his companions spotted a she-wolf and cubs along the bank and opened fire:

We reached the old wolf in time to watch a fierce green fire dying in her eyes. I realized then, and have known ever since, that there was something new to me in those eyes — something known only to her and to the mountain. I was young then and full of trigger itch; I thought that because fewer wolves meant more deer, then no wolves would mean a hunters' paradise. But after seeing the green fire die, I sensed that neither the wolf nor the mountain agreed with such a view. (Leopold, 1966, pp. 137–139)

The rest of Leopold's life was an extended meditation on that fierce green fire, how mountains think, and what both meant for humans.

Where Speer regarded himself as apolitical, Leopold regarded "biological education as a means of building citizens." (Leopold, 1966, p. 208). Instead of a deep naiveté about science, Leopold was scientific about science as few have ever been:

We are not scientists. We disqualify ourselves at the outset by professing loyalty to and affection for a thing: wildlife. A scientist in the old sense may have no loyalties except to abstractions, no affections except for his own kind.... The definitions of science written by, let us say, the National Academy, deal almost exclusively with the creation and exercise of power. But what about the creation and the exercise of wonder or respect for workmanship in nature? (Leopold, 1966; 1991, p. 276)

Where Speer aimed to escape "the demands of a world growing increasingly complicated," Leopold's approach to nature was hard-headed and practical:

The cultural value of wilderness boils down in the last analysis, to a question of intellectual humility. The shallow minded modern who has lost his rootage in the land assumes that he has already discovered what is important; it is such who prate of empires, political or economic that will last a thousand years. (Leopold, 1966, p. 279)

Where Speer had to learn his ethics in twenty years of confinement after the damage was done, Leopold learned his over a lifetime and laid the basis for an ecologically solvent land ethic. And where Speer's education made him immune from seeing or feeling tragedy unfolding around him, Leopold wrote:

One of the penalties of an ecological education is that one lives alone in a world of wounds. Much of the damage inflicted on land is quite invisible to laymen. An ecologist must either harden his shell and make believe that the consequences of science are none of his business, or he must be the doctor who sees the marks of death in a community that believes itself to be well and does not want to be told otherwise. (Leopold, 1966, p. 197)

After Speer and the Nazis, it has taken decades to undo the damage that could be undone. After Aldo Leopold, in contrast, it will take decades to fully grasp what he meant by a "land ethic," and considerably longer to make it a reality.

Dangers

From the lives of Speer and Leopold, what can be said about the dangers of formal education or schooling?

1. The first and overriding danger is that it will encourage young people to find careers before they find a suitable calling. A career is a job, a way to earn one's keep, a way to build a long resume, a ticket to somewhere else. For the upwardly mobile professionals, a career is too often a way to support a "lifestyle" by which one takes more than one gives back. In contrast, a calling has to do with one's larger purpose, personhood, deepest values, and the gift one wishes to give the world. A calling is about the use one makes of a career. A career is about specific aptitudes; a calling is about purpose. A career is planned with the help of "career development" specialists. A calling comes out of an inner conversation. A career can always be found in a calling, but a calling cannot easily be found in a career. The difference is roughly like deciding which end of the cart to attach the horse. Speer's problem was not a deficiency of mathematical skills, or reading ability, or computing ability, or logic narrowly conceived. I imagine that he would have done well on the SAT or Graduate Record Exam. His problem was simply that he had no calling that could bridle and channel his ambition. He simply wanted to "succeed" doing whatever it took. He was, as he says, "wild to accomplish," and ambition disconnected the alarm bells that should have sounded long before he saw blood on the floor in 1934. Speer was a careerist with no calling.

Leopold, on the other hand, found his calling as a boy in the marshes around Burlington and followed it wherever it took him. In time it took him a long way. From his boyhood interest in birds he went on in adult life to initiate the field of game management, organize the Wilderness Society, work actively on behalf of conservation throughout his lifetime, lay the groundwork for the field of environmental ethics, and still he found time to be a good teacher and father. There is a consistency and harmony to Leopold's life rather like a pilgrim following a vision.

2. A second danger of education is illustrated by a story told by British geographer, I.G. Simmons, of an early psychologist who distinguished between the sane and insane by placing those to be diagnosed together in a room with a series of spigots along one wall and mops and buckets along another. When the water was turned on, those he diagnosed as insane ran for the mops and buckets, while

the sane walked over and turned off the spigots. Conventional education produces lots of mop and bucket people who are educated to think as technicians think, which is to say, narrowly. The newspapers are full of mop and bucket proposals for this or that problem. But we need people now more than ever who think broadly and who understand systems, connecting patterns, and root causes.

The danger of formal schooling is that it works the other way, imprinting a disciplinary template onto impressionable minds and with it the belief that the world really is as disconnected as the typical curriculum with its divisions, disciplines, sub-disciplines. Students come to believe that there is such a thing as politics separate from ecology, or that economics has nothing to do with physics. But the world isn't this way, and except for the temporary convenience of analysis, it cannot be broken into disciplines and specializations without doing serious harm to the minds and lives of people who believe that it can be. We often forget to tell students that the convenience was temporary, and more seriously, we fail to show how things can be made whole again. One result is that students graduate without knowing how to think in whole systems, how to find connections, how to ask big questions, and how to separate trivial from the important. Not a few of them run for the mops and buckets all their lives.

I think this is a probable outcome of education conceived as the propagation of technical intelligence alone — what philosopher Mary Midgley calls the "cult of intelligence." In contrast to the whizkid type, Midgley describes what she calls "non-smart, but effective people" who:

> possess strong imaginative sensibility — the power to envisage possible goods that the world does not yet have and to see what is wrong with the world as it is. They are good at priorities, at comparing various goods, at asking what matters most. They have a sense of proportion, and a nose for the right directions. (Midgley, 1990, p. 41)

She is describing a kind of intellect that works slowly but comprehensively; a blend of good sense, moral acumen, and thorough knowledge. It is not necessarily the kind of intellect that always shows to good advantage on tests or on measures of IQ. And these are certainly not qualities that we solicit in SAT or GRE exams, nor are they ones that we typically associate with intelligence. But they happen to be the kind of intelligence that we will need a great deal of in the years ahead.

Speer in his Nazi years was a technician and a good one. His formal schooling gave him the tools which could be used by the Third Reich, but not the sense to ask why, and not the humanity necessary to recognize the face of barbarity when he saw it. Leopold, in contrast, began his career as something of a technician, but outgrew it. *A Sand County Almanac*, written shortly before his death, was nearly a perfect blend of science, natural history, and philosophy.

3. Third, there is the danger that education will damage the sense of wonder — the sheer joy in the created world — that is part of our original equipment at birth. It does this in various ways: by reducing learning to routines and memorization, by too many abstractions divorced from lived experience, by boring curriculum, by humiliation, by too many rules, by overstressing grades, by too much television and too many computers, by too much indoor learning, and mostly by deadening the feelings from which wonder grows. As the sense of wonder in nature diminishes, so too does our sense of the sacred, our pleasure in the created world, and the impulse behind a great deal of our best thinking. Where it is kept intact and growing, teachers need not worry about whether or not students learn reading, writing, and arithmetic.

In a small book titled *The Sense of Wonder*, Rachel Carson wrote that "it is not half so important to *know* as to *feel*" (Carson, 1984, p. 50). Feelings, she wrote, begin early in life in the exploration of nature, generally with the companionship of an adult. The sense of wonder is rooted in the trust that the world is, on balance, a friendly place full of interesting life "beyond the boundaries of human existence." The sense of wonder that Carson describes is not equivalent to a good science education, although in principle I see no reason why the two cannot be made compatible. I don't believe that wonder can be taught as "Wonder 101." If Carson is right it can only be felt and those early feelings must be encouraged, supported, and legitimized by a caring and knowledgeable adult. My hunch is that the sense of wonder is fragile; once crushed it rarely blossoms again but is replaced by varying shades of cynicism and disappointment in the world.

I know of no measures for wonder, but I think Speer lost his early on. His relation to nature prior to 1933 was, by his testimony, romantic and escapist. Thereafter he mentions it no more. To Speer, the adult, the natural world was not particularly wondrous, nor was it a source of insight, pleasure, or perspective. His orientation toward life, like that of the Nazi hierarchy, was necrophilic. Leopold, on the contrary, was a lifelong student of nature in the wild. By all accounts he was a remarkably astute observer of land which explains a great deal of his utter sanity and clarity of mind. Leopold's intellectual and spiritual anchor was not forged in a laboratory or library, but in time spent in the wild and in his later years in a run down farm he purchased that the family called "the shack."

Reconstruction: Organizing a Jailbreak

The dangers of education? I have described three that are particularly consequential for the way we live on the earth: (1) that formal education will cause students to worry about how to make a living before they know who they are; (2) that it will render them narrow technicians; and (3) that it will deaden their sense of wonder for the created world. Now, of course, education cannot do these things alone. It requires indifferent or absent parents, shopping malls, television — MTV — Nintendo, a culture aimed at the lowest common denominator, and deplaced people who do not know the very ground beneath their feet. Schooling is only an accomplice in a larger process of cultural decline. But no other institution is better able to reverse that decline. The answer, then, is not to abolish or diminish formal education, but rather to change it.

What can I propose instead? Alfred North Whitehead gave us the key to alternative life-centered education when he said that "First-hand knowledge is the ultimate basis of intellectual life. To a large extent book-learning conveys second-hand information" (Whitehead, 1967, p. 51). If we propose to educate young people to be ecologically literate, competent, and caring, we will have to provide an education that gives them first-hand knowledge of nature and the human role in it. The specifics will vary from place to place but the principle leads to two major changes in education. The first has to do with the architecture of schools, colleges, and universities, and their operational routines (Orr, 1991; Eagan & Orr, 1992). If schools and colleges were designed to give first-hand experience in nature, how would they be lighted, heated, landscaped, and designed?

The answers to these questions and related questions suggest making the school itself a laboratory patterned after ecological processes. They suggest policies governing energy, water, materials, food, architectural design, and waste aimed to maximize efficiency and replicate natural cycles. They suggest using institutional buying and investment power to help build sustainable local economies.

The second change implicit in Whitehead's logic would cause us to break down the walls that have been erected around the learning process. I am referring to walls of concrete as well as those made by clocks, bells, worn-out conceptions, procedural rules, and walls of a tired pedagogy erected in the belief that learning occurs only in prescribed times and places. I propose a jailbreak that puts learners of all ages out-of-doors more often in well conceived experiences with rivers, marshes, woods, fields, mountains, animals, clearcuts, feedlots, dumps, sewage plants, mines, oil spills, and power plants. At Oberlin College, for example, students are working with local conservation groups and the Environmental Protection Agency to help clean up the local watershed. They are establishing historical baseline data, conducting biological surveys, monitoring pollution, attending meetings, working with local health officials. In the future they will work with farmers on problems of non-point runoff, low-input agriculture, and establishment of riparian forests. They could have learned the same material in a classroom, but its impact would not have been the same, and they would not have learned that they can change things.

The requirements of first-hand knowledge also suggest going on to the acquisition of ecological competence. Whitehead again:

> There is a co-ordination of senses and thought, and also a reciprocal influence between brain activity and material creative activity. It is a moot point whether the human hand created the human brain, or the brain created the hand. Certainly the connection is intimate and reciprocal. (Whitehead, 1967, p. 50)

In other words, thinking and doing reinforce each other and best occur together. Yet modern pedagogy, which begins at the neck and works up, consigns "material creative activity" to vo-tech schools far removed from the liberal arts. By Whitehead's logic, the liberal arts are not liberal enough. Applied to ecological education, a more liberal liberal arts would include the sustainable practice of agriculture, forestry, solar technology, restoration ecology, and ecological engineering which combine practical competence with intellectual development.

I think it is time to begin to experiment with more radical ideas. For example, some tribal cultures required that their youth go through a rite of passage into adulthood by sending them into the wilderness for a time to test their person and character and help them find their place in the cosmos. These were risky trials requiring stamina, courage, and competence. Perhaps we should consider reinstating the practice as a requirement for passage into adult life.

A national program patterned on Outward Bound that would place young people in wilderness or remote areas for a summer would do more to bond young people to the earth than any amount of classroom experiences.

A second possibility is the establishment of mentoring and apprenticeship programs that attach young people for a time to persons who have demonstrated a high degree of ecological competence, courage, and creativity. These might include farmers, foresters, ranchers, restoration ecologists, urban ecologists, landscape planners, naturalists, and environmental activists. We think that education has to do with the association of young people with others who are intellectually adept. I believe that this ought to be supplemented by developing more extensive opportunities to learn directly from those who have demonstrated competence and who have in one way or another paid a price for their convictions. This too is first-hand knowledge.

Conclusion

There is a national consensus that American education is failing. In one view the measures of failure are those indicators showing a decline in our economic competitiveness. By another, less acknowledged standard, the marks of failure are the signs of ecological decay, desolation, and blight spreading across the face of the earth. In some ways these two measures report the same things: the decline in concern for the future and dishonest bookkeeping both economic and ecological. But the solutions each side proposes vary widely. The goal of short-term economic competitiveness leads some educational reformers to propose more gee-whiz technologies in the classroom, more economically useful courses in science, math, and business, national standards aimed to make our young people, in Douglas Strong's words, "little virtuosos of calculation and competition." The other path is much harder to render into programmatic form, but its aim is an education that teaches what one can imagine the earth would teach us if only it could: Listening and silence; Thousand year cycles; How to think like a mountain; Humility; Holiness of the Earth; The limits of mind; The connectedness of all life; Courtesy toward animals; Beauty; Celebration; Wilderness; Giving; Restoration; and Obligation.

References

Carson, R. (1984). *The sense of wonder*. New York: Harper.

Eagan, D., & Orr, D. (1992). *The campus and environmental responsibility*. San Francisco: Jossey-Bass.

Leopold, A. (1966). *A Sand County Almanac*. New York: Ballantine.

McLuhan, T. C. (1971). *Touch the earth: A self-portrait of Indian existence*. New York: Simon & Schuster.

Midgley, M. (1990). Why smartness is not enough. In M. Clark and S. Wawrytko (Eds.), *Rethinking the curriculum*. Westport, CT: Greenwood Press.

Orr, D.W. (1991). *Ecological literacy: Education and the transition to a postmodern world*. Albany: State University of New York Press.

Snyder, G. (1990). *The practice of the wild*. San Francisco: North Point Press.

Speer, A. (1970). *Inside the Third Reich*. Boston: Houghton Mifflin.

Whitehead, A. N. (1967). *The aims of education*. New York: Free Press.

Whicher, S. E. (Ed.). (1957). *Selections from Ralph Waldo Emerson*. Boston: Houghton Mifflin.

Chapter 2

Implications of the Ecological Crisis for the Reform of Teacher Education

C. A. Bowers

What is perceived as newsworthy has changed radically over the last decade. Typical of this change is that in 1979 the *New York Times* relegated to page 42 an account of how human activity was changing the earth's atmosphere; in 1988 a piece on the same environmental problems (now called the "greenhouse effect") appeared on page 1. Journals such as *Scientific American* and *The Economist* recently devoted special issues to laying out the most critical dimensions of the ecological crisis. Reports by world commissions, scientific bodies (U.S. National Academy of Science's *One Earth, One Future* being the latest), and independent research groups like The Worldwatch Institute have succeeded in alerting large segments of the American public to the fact that our cultural practices are seriously threatening the life-sustaining capabilities of natural systems. Although there is not scientific agreement on whether we have irreversibly crossed critical thresholds, there is agreement on the trendlines: The expectations and demands of the world's cultures represent a sharply accelerating upward curve while the degradation of soils, water, forests, atmosphere, and species diversity reflects an accelerating downward curve.

Except for deep ecology writers, most accounts of the ecological crisis present data on changes in the environment, urge that legislative action be taken to correct the damaging practices, and essentially remain silent on the cultural aspects of the problem. That is, they do not recognize that the cultural assumptions underlying our beliefs, values, and practices may be the most critical part of the problem needing to be addressed. This same silence on the connection between cultural beliefs and the ecological crisis also characterizes, with only minor exceptions, the national journals and professional meetings of educators.

An examination of paper topics at the last three meetings of the American Educational Research Association is a good indicator that the ecological crisis has not influenced the concerns of the mainstream of professional educators. The AERA *Handbook on Research and Teaching* (1986) is further evidence. It contains reviews of hundreds of research articles covering a wide range of topics ("Teacher's Thought Processes," "Teacher Behavior and Student Achievement," "Classroom Discourse," and so forth) but there are no references to how curricular content and teacher decision making may contribute to students adopting taken-for-granted attitudes toward cultural patterns of thinking that are putting demands on the habitat that cannot be sustained over the long term — and perhaps not even over the shorter term of a few decades. I suspect that my own experience, at the more local level of reforming a teacher education program, is not atypical of the field; although I kept urging that the ecological crisis be taken into account in reframing the theoretical foundations of our new approach to the professional education of teachers, it was totally disregarded in the final outcome. I mention this here because later in the article I want to suggest some strategically important steps that must be taken if we are to begin helping teachers understand how the cultural beliefs and patterns they reinforce in the classroom may be contributing to the ecological crisis — even as they teach students to understand and respect the fragile character of natural systems, and to recycle paper, plastics, and so forth.

An important reason that accounts both for cultural patterns that ignore the sustaining capacity of the habitat, and for the silence on the relevance of the culture/ecological crisis for rethinking our approach to the professional education of teachers, is that fundamental aspects of the dominant mindset are based on the achievements of thinkers who laid the foundations of modern science and liberal political institutions. Though subsequent generations made important refinements in what can be loosely termed "Cartesianism," the 17th century thinkers left a legacy with several distinct characteristics that make it difficult both to recognize that the destruction of the habitat will eventually lead to the demise of the culture, and to understand the influence of culture on their own language and thought processes. The achievements of Cartesian thought, now manifested in computers and other mechanical and social techniques, originally represented a response to a totally different set of social issues and circumstances, but it continues to be the main conceptual framework of today's society — including the field of teacher education. Thus, it is important to identify the most salient characteristics that contribute to our inability to address the cultural aspects of the crisis of the diverging cultural and environmental trendlines.

The most fundamental aspects of this mindset include a special way of thinking about the nature of knowledge, individualism, language, and change. Briefly, they can be summarized as the myth that knowledge is the result of a thinking process that occurs in the head of an individual; the myth that autonomy (freedom) is the realization of the individual's fullest potential (to be self-determining); the myth that language is a neutral conduit (individuals put their ideas into words and get them across to someone else); the myth that "man" is separate from nature; and the myth that change, when rationally directed, is progressive (in its current form of expression any form of change often is viewed as progressive). These myths can be seen as underpinning cultural practices ranging from representing computers as a neutral technology that facilitates progress in the "Information Age" to classroom techniques such as "mastery teaching." What the myths put out of focus are the encoding processes that make up the patterns of a culture, and how these patterns are reenacted — even by individuals who consider themselves to be thinking in a culture-free way. For educators who still think within this mindset (and most institutions and higher education still reinforce it) the connections between cultural, linguistic, and thought patterns are usually not considered. Nor are they likely to ask whether the cultural patterns reinforced through classroom techniques are part of the ecological solution or problem. Rational experimental thought, supported by data, as Descartes, Bacon, as well as more recent positivistic thinkers attempted to show, is the basis of human progress. Until recently the upward trendline was considered as the expression of progress and the natural outcome of a rationally, technologically based culture; there seemed to be no need to take account of the condition of the habitat because there appeared to be an endless supply of new territories and exploitable resources to sustain the myth of man as a unique being in the universe, with a special destiny.

These myths unleashed unique expressions of cultural energy, particularly in the areas of technology, economics, and the arts — with many achievements that are desirable and, hopefully, long lasting. But the basic reference point for judging the adequacy of the assumptions (myths) that underlie the practices and sense of vision of a culture is whether it is sustainable over the long haul. That is, does it meet the ultimate test suggested by Lester R. Brown and Sandra Postel (1987) that "a sustainable society satisfies its needs without diminishing the prospects of the next generation?" When judged against this criterion, where we are witnessing a third of our topsoil disappear, major aquifers being depleted at an accelerating rate, alarming rates of deforestation, and the build up of carbon dioxide in the atmosphere, we need to ask whether the Cartesian based mindset that has produced the seeming miracle of modernization has to be replaced by a more ecologically responsive set of cultural beliefs. With experts arguing whether we have 40, 60, or even 100 years before recoverable sources of crude oil are exhausted — to cite just one area of our depleted environment — it would seem that the obvious answer is "yes."

We cannot change a culture in the same way we obtain a consumer item off the shelf, or acquire a new technique for solving a classroom problem. Nor is culture like a machine where an out-worn part can be replaced or retrofitted with a new innovation; rather it evolves over time and its past patterns are often part of present practices and beliefs. It's also an aspect of everything we think and do, but the patterns are often unrecognized because we have internalized them as part of our natural attitude. The Cartesian mindset, which represents the individual as free of the influence of culture, makes the presence of cultural patterns in our experience even more difficult to recognize. In addition to the problem of being aware of our own culturally influenced patterns, there is an even more complex set of questions relating to the kind of patterns we need to evolve, and whether the new ecologically sustainable patterns can take account of the genuine advances we have made in the areas of civil liberties, the arts, and science/technology. These questions I suspect will be at the center of a discussion that will take on a greater sense of urgency as different social groups recognize they cannot isolate themselves from the consequences of the ecological crisis. Even as this debate goes on in the larger society, it is possible to see steps that can be taken in the area of teacher education that can contribute to a more ecologically responsive form of education in the classroom, and to bringing our own guiding assumptions into line with the emerging awareness that we cannot continue to have progress while the sustaining capacity of the habitat declines.

A first step is to identify a way of thinking that overcomes the dualisms (man and nature, mind and body, and knower and known) that characterize the Cartesian mindset. The new way of thinking must also take account of the tacit character of most of our cultural knowledge, as well as the influence of language on thought. The ideas of Gregory Bateson avoid these dualisms and thus could serve as part of the foundation for a more ecologically responsive way of thinking. As demonstrated in *Responsive Teaching: An Ecological Approach to Classroom Patterns of Culture, Language, and Thought* (Bowers & Flinders, 1990), the use of Bateson's conceptual framework helps us understand humans as part of an ecology (as opposed to the Cartesian view that man must dominate nature through rationally based techniques), and to take account of the different cultures that are increasingly represented in the ecology of the classroom. In effect, his ideas help illuminate how the curriculum may be reinforcing in the minds of students cultural myths that underpinned the Industrial Revolution that was based on the ecologically disastrous idea that nature must be exploited in order for humans to progress. It is also important to note that his essential ideas are compatible with such areas of inquiry as the sociology of knowledge, social and cultural linguistics, and the insights now emerging from the studies into the metaphorical nature of language and thought — all areas essential to understanding how culture is transmitted (and mediated) in the classroom.

As anyone who has read *Steps to an Ecology of Mind* (1972) and *Mind and Nature* (1980) can attest, Bateson is not easily understood on the first reading, or even the second reading. It's not that he is a poor writer or that his readers are unintelligent. Rather, I suspect it has more to do with a point he makes about conceptual maps and territory. That is, most people in the dominant culture have acquired a natural attitude toward the pattern of thinking that characterizes the Cartesian mindset. Bateson provides a fundamentally different conceptual map that enables us to recognize different aspects of the territory (field of experience) than what the Cartesian conceptual map puts in focus. In order to understand Bateson to the point where we can expand on his ideas by relating them to the process of cultural transmission and intercultural communication in the classroom, we first have to recognize how previously held Cartesian assumptions still may be directing — and thus limiting — our understanding. To put it succinctly, Bateson will not make sense to a Cartesian thinker.

Space here does not allow for a full explanation of Bateson's position, or for a full analysis of the changes in our approach to teacher education that would follow from taking his ideas seriously. Instead, I shall focus on key ideas that seem especially relevant to laying the basis for a way of thinking about curricular issues that relate directly to the ecological crisis. By considering the implications of these curricular issues for what teachers need to understand about the culture–language–thought connection, we shall be addressing some of the implications of a Batesonian framework for the reform of teacher education.

Bateson's long experience doing anthropological field work, studying communication processes among animals, and working on the problem of schizophrenia — to cite just a few of the areas in which he made lasting contributions — led him to focus on the patterns and relationships that characterize a group. This approach, which focuses on the importance of interactions as the basis of information exchange (communicating with another person, a person cutting down a tree, a person drinking water that has an unusual color and taste, etc.), leads to a fundamentally different way of understanding the mental process; it also leads to reforming how we think about the individual. Whereas the Cartesian tradition leads to viewing the thought process as individually centered (person observes an external world and events and thinks about them, or just thinks and ignores the external world), Bateson argues that the mental processes are actually quite different. First, he holds that the most elementary form of idea or bit of information is a "difference which makes a difference." That is, the contacts between the different entities (humans, plants, soil, atmosphere, etc.) that characterize the multiple layers of life that constitute an ecology involve differences in patterns. These differences, which are bits of information exchanged as the patterns of one entity (e.g., a person speaking to someone else), lead to adjustments in response as the changes in the other person's patterns (differences in tone of voice, body language, etc.) are taken into account.

Instead of viewing the individual as mentally autonomous, Bateson states that the "individual mind is immanent but not only in the body. It is immanent also in the pathways and messages outside the body..." (1972, p. 461). The way in which information is exchanged through the pathways that connect the changing patterns characterizing membership in an ecology is illustrated in the process of cutting down a tree. The self-correcting mental process, where thought is modified by changes (differences that make a difference) in the interactive patterns, is illustrated in Bateson's example of felling a tree with an axe. "The self-corrective (i.e., mental) process," as he describes it, involves differences in the surface of the tree caused by previous strokes" — (differences in retina)–(differences in brain)–(difference in muscles)–(difference in movement of axe)–(difference in tree), etc." The total system, to stay with this example, of information exchanges has the "characteristics of immanent mind" (1972, p. 317).

As the individual is always part of a larger set of interactive relationships, Bateson wants to emphasize the importance of recognizing that the well being of individuals is interdependent (over the long term) with the viability of the system (ecology) of which they are a part. As he puts it, "Thus, in no system which shows mental characteristics can any part have unilateral control over the whole. In other words, *the mental characteristics of the system are immanent, not in some part, but in the system as a whole*" (1972, p. 316). To put it another way, the mental processes that have their roots in cultural traditions may lead to dumping toxic wastes into the environment, leading to changes in the patterns of water, plant, and animal life that will eventually impact human behavior. The totality of information exchanges that occur within a living ecology, where humans are ultimately interdependent with the rest of the biota, become for Bateson the basic unit of survival (1972, p. 483).

While Bateson argues that humans are participants in a larger mental ecology, he acknowledges that humans make sense of the information exchanges in a very unique way — and this is where everything comes together in terms of discussing the relevance of Bateson's ideas for reforming teacher education in a way that takes account of the ecological crisis. Humans, he points out, make sense of the information exchanges (and ignore a great deal of it) on the basis of the conceptual images and schemata they acquire from their culture. That is, human thinking is metaphorical, and the root metaphors of a culture that influence the process of analogic thinking (which is always involved in understanding new situations) provide a schema that may prevent certain forms of information from being recognized or properly understood.

The root metaphors of Western culture have included the image of a "man"-centered universe, and with the emergence of Cartesian thinking, it was overlaid with the powerful image of a mechanical-like universe. Since these root metaphors put out of focus how humans are interdependent members of a larger ecology, information flowing through the pathways of the biota — changes in chemistry and soil, water, air, as well as the loss of species — was not recognized by people until recently when Rachel Carson and Aldo Leopold sounded the alarm that our cultural practices and beliefs were threatening the environment. People were rational but within the conceptual boundaries of these deeply rooted cultural metaphors. We could cite other examples of how culturally based metaphorical schemata cut us from or distort the flow of information that characterizes the adjustments occurring within the larger cultural/natural system: the metaphorical image of technology as neutral has caused us to ignore the cultural orientations reinforced through educational computing, the image of the individual as autonomous has put out of focus the information exchanges that characterize membership in a larger community, and the schema of thinking that represents change as progressive has helped to limit our understanding of the many ways we reenact and build upon traditions. As Bateson points out, the map is not the territory. The two problems that may arise are that a person or society may think that what they are aware of (actually, what their culturally acquired schemata allows them to be aware of) is an accurate representation of the world, and the culturally derived schemata of understanding may distort fundamental relationships — like the belief that humans can survive and progress through even greater reliance on technological solutions.

To summarize the essential ideas of Bateson: Rather than viewing the individual as an autonomous and reflective being, we should focus on the person as an interactive member of a larger ecology; the mental characteristics of the entire system tell us more about its viability than what we can learn from considering the actions and thoughts of individuals; the conceptual mapping process of humans (making sense of the information exchanges) may lead to interpretations and subsequent actions that threaten the self-correcting capacity of the system and lead to stress and decline.

Bateson's ecological model seems especially relevant to understanding the classroom as an interactive system of patterns and relationships — with the teacher and students continually responding to changes in each other's patterns of behavior and thought process. Use of a different tone of voice, the longer than usual pause, the telling of an event in an episodic rather than topic-centered linear manner, the establishment of eye contact and a smile, the use of an unusual word, and so forth, characterize the classroom as an ecology of ongoing relationships. These relationships are, to use his phrase, the pathways through which information is communicated.

When we take account that body language, use of space, metaphorical language, participation patterns, and so forth, often reflect the primary culture of both students and teachers, we can begin to see that many of the professional judgments of the teacher should be based on an understanding of how the culture of the student influences the multiple dimensions of communication in the classroom. On the one hand, Bateson's ecological model takes us in the direction of seeing the implications of teachers having a deep knowledge of cultures (particularly how the student's primary culture may be the source of the patterns, which may be individually interpreted by students, that may influence communication), as well as understanding forms of communication other than spoken and written discourse.

The other direction Bateson's ecological model takes us has to do with the relationship between the content of the curriculum and the ecological crisis. In the most basic sense, the ecological crisis — polluted water and air, overuse of soils and aquifers, loss of vegetation and species diversity — has been an unrecognized part of most people's experiences. That is, the changes in habitat have been signalled through the information pathways for years. In more severe situations people responded to the "difference which makes a difference" by using more pesticides to control pests, fertilizers to compensate for loss of soil nutrients, chemicals to purify the water, drilling deeper wells — and when all else failed, moving on to habitats that were still viable. The conceptual maps, which represents the dominant cultural group's way of knowing, contributed to focusing on technological development and progress in conveniences and consumer goods. Thus the impact of cultural practices on the sustaining capacity of natural systems tended not to be recognized.

With scientific studies yielding a picture of serious habitat disruption, with even more coming if the world population doubles as expected over the next 25 to 30 years, it becomes increasingly difficult to ignore the fact that the most important issues facing educators have to do with the cultural beliefs and values students are socialized to accept as part of their natural attitude. In Bateson's terms, we have to ask whether the conceptual maps we are reinforcing students to accept (mostly at the unconscious level) are adequate for making the transition to a lifestyle that is more in ecological balance. An examination of textbooks and other curriculum materials suggests the dimensions of the problem we face in the professional education of teachers. Aside from instruction on recycling (mostly elementary and middle grades) and discussions of environmental policies in some high schools (along with the biology class approach to studying natural systems), students will encounter a curriculum that is based on an anthropocentric view of the universe. This is expressed in references to the environment as "our world," "our resources," and by framing issues and values in terms of a human perspective that is generally linked to consumerism. Other aspects of the culture being made problematic by the ecological crisis include how progress, individualism, community, science, and technology are represented in curriculum materials. Some textbooks are beginning to provide a more complex way of thinking about the relationships previously mapped in much narrower terms by these cultural metaphors. But the content of the curriculum is only part of the problem.

What seems more relevant to providing the different forms of knowledge essential for living an ecologically sustainable life, given our responsibility for the education of teachers, is the teacher's own understanding of the following: the nature of the ecological crisis, the interconnection of cultures and habitat, and how culture is reproduced through the language processes under the teacher's control during the process of primary socialization.

A strong case can be made that culture is the medium of the classroom (including both the content and processes of communication, with variations in individualized interpretations and expression), and that understanding its complexity and diversity should be as foundational to the professional education of teachers as human anatomy is to doctors, and the Constitution to lawyers. The accelerating rate of environmental disruption now causing informed people to take seriously the question of whether the planet can be saved for the generations that will follow makes it imperative that we finally recognize what is involved in education, namely the introduction of youth into the patterns of the culture. And the problem posed by the ecological crisis is whether the cultural patterns — in ways of thinking, uses of technology, and "exploitation of natural resources" — make as much sense today.

The cultural basis of the teacher's professional knowledge includes far more, and probably a very different slant, than what would be the main preoccupations of academic anthropologists. Anthropologists, for example — at least that aspect of their work that gets to be part of an education and anthropology course — tend not to focus on the question of how a culture lives within the sustaining capacity of the natural habitat. Nor do they, as a rule, recognize the role that metaphorical thinking plays in the thought processes of a cultural group. In suggesting that teachers need a better understanding of culture, I am not arguing that the addition of a course in anthropology and education to the teacher education curriculum will solve the problem — but it would be a useful step.

What seems more central to understanding the nature of cultural patterns, and to asking whether they are likely to contribute further to the cultural myth that humans can progress while the sustaining capabilities of the habitat decline, is the metaphorical nature of all thought and the process of primary socialization. Most teachers are educated to view language as a conduit into which people put their ideas and data for transmission to the listener or reader. Space does not allow for a full explanation of the constitutive role that metaphor plays in the thought process, but I would like to mention just a few characteristics that will bring the discussion back to Bateson's point that the thought process is always part of a larger mental ecology (which includes, for him, both the cultural and natural environment). Briefly, teachers use analogues as the basis for introducing new concepts; the new, in a sense, is understood in terms of the familiar. The process of metaphorical thinking helps to illuminate similarities (e.g., computers process data like the mind does, the "President is like a quarterback," etc.) while hiding differences. The analogue is selected on the basis of a root metaphor shared at a taken-for-granted level by the dominant cultural group; actually, the root metaphor (e.g., the mechanistic view of the universe — including the human mind) influences the choice of analogue. These aspects of metaphor are becoming more widely recognized but have not influenced the educational mainstream to give up its preoccupation with viewing thought as individualistic.

Metaphorical thinking also occurs when students hear teachers use such words as "individualism," "progress," "data," "technology," and so forth. These are iconic metaphors that encode an earlier stage of analogic thinking, where a root metaphor as well as previous processes of analogic thinking leave their influence on the schema or template that is the basis of understanding.

For example, recognizing the thought processes (analogic thinking) that constituted the taken-for-granted understanding of "intelligence" for several generations of educators helps illuminate how a word encodes the metaphorical thinking of earlier generations. To put it another way, and this is Bateson's point, language encodes the mental processes of earlier times. For the teacher who is continually providing students with the vocabulary for understanding new areas of the culture covered by the curriculum, as well as a vocabulary for thinking about taken-for-granted aspects of daily experience, the words that encode earlier processes of metaphorical thinking represent what should be a continuing series of professional judgments. But these judgments are seldom made in a clear, informed manner — since few teachers have been educated to understand how language thinks us as we think within the language. Nor are teachers generally able to recognize the root metaphors that organize thought (and the person's taken-for-granted attitudes) into patterns that serve as the basis of social life — including how we view the environment.

A good test of whether my argument holds up would be to investigate the view of language most teachers hold, whether they are able to identify the root metaphors of the dominant culture (e.g., how anthropocentrism is represented in curriculum materials) and how they may differ from the root metaphors of other cultural groups represented in the classroom, and how they understand the language–thought connection. My encounters with teachers and the professional literature strongly suggests that few teachers would recognize how the conceptual maps being constituted through the classroom curriculum may be preparing students to think about the current crisis in terms of the metaphorical language that underpinned the Industrial Revolution.

The dynamics of primary socialization is also essential for teachers to understand, as it represents the moment of vulnerability when the student is acquiring the language for thinking about a new (for them) area of shared cultural life. It is a very complex process involving taken-for-granted beliefs, the language–thought connection, points of potential confusion about whether the content should be understood as factual or as an interpretation, the problem of empowerment which may be interpreted differently depending upon the cultural groups represented in the classroom, and now the critical issue of whether the content of primary socialization contributes to a form of cultural existence that meets the test of living in ecological balance. Like the use of metaphors, primary socialization is what teachers do. If they do not understand the process, students, society, and the environment may suffer from the passing on of a metaphorical language and taken-for-granted beliefs that are now inadequate.

Both the use of metaphorical language and primary socialization involve understanding the continually changing patterns and relationships which make up the mental and social ecology of the classroom. Unfortunately, the Cartesian mindset (itself a distinct cultural tradition with its own metaphorical language) has been dominant in teacher education. The result has been an emphasis on the use of techniques, viewing the student in terms of behavior, and reducing learning to behavioral outcomes. The concern with a culturally responsive approach to teacher education, and now with being ecologically responsive as well, brings up the fundamentally important issue of how to bring about changes in teacher education programs where either (and sometimes both) a technicist approach prevails among faculty or there is a commitment to thinking of teacher education within the liberal framework of the autonomous individual. As a member of a faculty that combines both, I have learned a few lessons over a twenty year period about the politics of educational reform.

Since publishing *Cultural Literacy for Freedom* in 1974, I have attempted to introduce a cultural/language perspective into our teacher education program and to ground it in an understanding of professional decision making surrounding the dynamics of primary socialization. The argument for this, in addition to scholarly evidence, was that the ecological crisis brings into question the cultural traditions being taught in the schools. Without going into the history of my own institution, I would like to conclude with a few recommendations that emerge from my experience in a teacher education program that is supposed to be in one of the more environmentally conscious states. Given the academic tradition that upholds faculty autonomy to pursue any line of inquiry and to treat competing paradigms as equal, I have found that it is nearly impossible to have a sustained discussion about critical social issues, such as the question of whether the ecological crisis has implications for teacher education. These issues may be raised by faculty members, but if there is no strong administrative support and subsequent leadership in keeping the issue alive, it will remain "only one of many equally important issues" — which is the liberal way of dismissing it. If a faculty can discuss the implications of the ecological crisis and reach some consensus on whether it should be given a high priority, it is then essential that the faculty hold the administrator accountable for keeping it as an agreed-upon priority before the faculty. My experience has been that if social issues, like the ecological crisis, concern only a few faculty, they then tend to get associated with personality traits. The issue has to be owned by the majority of faculty, and then the administrator should provide leadership in keeping alive the collective memory and commitment.

To summarize: The easiest and most powerful way for helping teachers recognize how culture, in its many forms of expression, relates to the problem of environmental sustainability is to introduce them to a deep understanding of the culture–language–thought connection. A broader understanding of the encoding process of metaphor, particularly its relation to the root metaphors of a cultural group and how it guides understanding (the "information pathways," to use Bateson's phrase) will help teachers recognize how the culture–language–thought connection relates to the content of the formal curriculum, as well as the student's own cultural traditions. It might also help to sensitize teachers to their own taken-for-granted attitudes toward language — where, in terms of the gender issue, we have seen real progress. A second area that needs to be incorporated into teacher education is an understanding of the dynamics of primary socialization with special attention being given to those aspects of the process where teacher decision making may have a long term influence on the student's thought process. Other steps include the introduction of courses that address how to develop more ecologically responsive curriculum materials, as well as courses that introduce teachers to the patterns of cultures that have evolved in a more ecologically balanced manner.

If we take seriously the influence of culture and language on thought, and begin to rethink those aspects of our symbolic world that are contributing to the ecological crisis, there will be other changes — both incremental and major — that go beyond the initial steps suggested here. But given the amount of media coverage on the scope and seriousness of habitat abuse, I am concerned with how long it is taking for the teaching profession to begin addressing this cultural issue.

References

Bateson, G. (1972). *Steps to an ecology of mind*. New York: Ballantine.

Bateson, G. (1980). *Mind and nature: A necessary uniting*. New York: Bantam.

Bowers, C. A. (1974). Cultural literacy for freedom. Eugene, OR: Elan.

Bowers, C. A., & Flinders, D.J. (1990). *Responsive teaching: An ecological approach to classroom patterns of language, culture, and thought*. New York: Teachers College Press.

Brown, L., & Postel, S. (1987). "Thresholds of change." In Linda Starke (Ed.), *State of the world 1987*. New York: Norton.

Silver, S. S., & Defries, R.S. (1990). *One earth, one future: Our changing global environment*. Washington, DC: National Academy Press.

Wittrock, M. C. (Ed.). (1986). *Handbook in research on teaching*, 3rd ed. New York: Macmillan.

Chapter 3

Worldviews, Educational Orientations, and Holistic Education

John P. Miller

Michael Fullan (1991), an authority in curriculum implementation, argues that curriculum changes involve practices, resources, and beliefs. Of the three factors, beliefs are the most difficult to define and to articulate. Since the publication of a book that I co-authored (Miller & Seller, 1985), I have been working with teachers and school administrators to help them clarify their educational beliefs in various contexts. Another term for educational beliefs is *orientation* to curriculum which involves a basic stance towards teaching and learning. It includes several factors such as a view of the teacher, the child, and the learning process. In an earlier work (Miller, 1983) I outlined seven orientations (e.g., subject, developmental, behavioral, cognitive process, social, humanistic, and transpersonal), but after working with these seven I found that they could be naturally grouped into three larger orientations or positions of transmission, transaction, and transformation. My experience is that these positions are helpful to individuals and school staffs in clarifying their own beliefs about programs and learning environments. In short, the orientations are crucial to building an educational vision. People from other professions such as law and medicine have also found the positions helpful in clarifying how to approach such issues as legal education (Kent, 1991). The positions can be applied beyond education because each position is rooted in a worldview. This worldview can permeate all phases of thought and practice. In the pages that follow I describe these three positions and explore how they can help us clarify the nature of holistic education. Each position is connected to philosophy, psychology, economics, and of course, education.

Transmission Position

The underlying world view of the transmission position is atomism, as the universe is conceived of small reducible units.

This atomism underlies analytic philosophy, behavioral psychology, and laissez-faire economics. William Barrett (1979) states that analytic philosophy is "a kind of philosophical analysis that proceeds by the piecemeal decomposition of any complex subject into its logically ultimate components" (p. 36). Bertrand Russell actually led a school of thought called "logical atomism." Russell's view was that not only language, but reality itself, is composed of "logical atoms." Barrett summarizes:

> ... the world must ultimately be made up of atomic facts that correspond to the atomic statements with which logical analysis terminates. And the various groupings of these atomic facts make up the complex facts that constitute our experience. We thus arrive at the full-fledged doctrine of logical atomism. (p. 39)

Philosophy, in this century, has abandoned metaphysics, which is now the domain of subatomic physicists, who wonder at the remarkable behavior of subatomic particulars. Like most academic disciplines in this century, philosophy became a pseudoscience. Traditionally, philosophy had been a struggle to discover and *to live* the good or virtuous life. Socrates is probably the best example of this quest. Kaplan summarizes the dichotomy of the present-day philosopher when he states: "What [the analytic philosopher] identifies as philosophy is not something that he lives by, but a purely intellectual pursuit, like the study of mathematics or physics with which it is so intimately associated" (p. 88).

Because the worldview of the analytic philosopher is made up of isolated segments that may or may not be related to each other, these philosophers focus on science, observations, inference, clarity, and precision. Art, beauty, ethics, and spirituality are separate and unrelated realms. This separation between rational and intuitive modes of thought, of course, is not confined to analytic philosophy; it has tended to dominate most of academia and has permeated educational philosophy and psychology throughout most of this century, whereas other currents, such as existentialism and humanistic psychology, have generally been isolated from the academic mainstream. In short, analytic philosophy has reinforced the schizoid split that separates head from heart in our culture.

This same dichotomy is apparent in the present-day back-to-basics movement — an approach to curriculum that exemplifies the transmission position. This movement advocates reducing the curriculum to basic elements (e.g., the three Rs), each of which is taught separately. Of course there are different strands of thought within the back-to-basics movement, but generally it is consistent with the transmission position in that it breaks down the curriculum into small segments that are unrelated and cut off from the affective and spiritual dimensions of life.

Perhaps there is no better example of atomism than in behavioral psychology. Thorndike (1913), a behaviorist, made a revealing statement about problem solving when he wrote that "a person whose general aim is to solve a mechanical puzzle may hit upon the solution, or some part of it, in the course of random fumbling, may hit upon it sooner in the next trial and so progress in the learning — all with little help from ideas about the puzzle or his own movements" (p. 131). If the universe is composed of unconnected atoms then problem solving is no more than random fumbling. With this view of problem solving, Thorndike's successor, B.F. Skinner, developed highly controlled learning environments to insure that the learners developed the desired behavior. In behavioral learning, units are broken down into the smallest components and put in sequence as in programmed learning texts. Clearly, this view of learning leaves no room for creativity or synthesis.

Finally, laissez-faire economics is atomistic at its core. Heilbroner (1980) characterizes the world of Adam Smith in this way:

> The world of Adam Smith has been called a world of atomistic competition; a world in which no agent of the productive mechanism on the side of labor or capital was powerful enough to interfere with or to resist the pressures of competition. It was a world in which each agent was forced to scurry after its self-interest in a vast social free-for-all. (p. 56)

In Smith's atomistic world people are only connected through the marketplace where they buy and sell goods and services. Milton Friedman has taken up the mantle of Smith and uses an interesting metaphor to characterize the laissez-faire world. Friedman (1962) states: "In its simplest form, such a society consists of a number of independent households — a collection of Robinson Crusoes as it were" (p. 13). The transmission view of society is one of people operating in isolation, unconnected to each other. The extreme end of this position is where the atoms are seen as hostile and we become survivalists waiting for the worst to happen. The survivalist's world is one of total paranoia, where Crusoe's household is permeated with fear and anger.

Educationally, the transmission position has a long history and has two strands. One strand is the behavioral, while the other has focussed on students studying the standard subjects taught in a traditional style (e.g., lecture and recitation). In either case the relationship between the curriculum and child can be characterized in the following diagram:

In the behavioral strand this relationship is known as stimulus–response, S–R, while in the traditional subject curriculum the teacher or text conveys information to the student. In both cases there is essentially a one-way flow or transmission of skills and knowledge. There is little or no opportunity to reflect or analyze the information.

Examples of transmission curriculum are abundant. Most of our schooling is conducted in this form. Students sit in rows and study from the textbook or worksheet. Evaluation tends to focus on information recall or performing low level skills. Today, much of the so-called restructuring, or school reform, is still attempting to implement a transmission curriculum so that student test scores compare better with scores of students in other countries. Nobody ever asks what these scores measure. In most cases they don't measure anything important, such as high level thinking skills or student self-concept, because these elements are very difficult to assess. The general thrust of this reform is to improve student skills so that he or she can become a better Robinson Crusoe so that his or her country can "compete" in the world marketplace.

Not all transmission education is negative. There are times when skills are best learned by being broken down into their components or when information is best conveyed by a short lecture. However, as a total educational approach, the transmission view of education is a very narrow and limiting one. The student is seen as passive and not really capable of making intelligent choices or having affective and spiritual needs. I will discuss the relationship of the transmission position to holistic education later in this paper.

Transaction Position

From the transaction position the universe is seen as rational and intelligible. The atoms are now linked in a linear fashion.

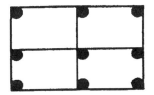

The underlying worldview is the *scientific method*. In the transaction position the student is seen as rational, being capable of making intelligent decisions based on some form of the scientific method. This view was summarized by Dewey (1938/1969) when he said that the scientific method is

> the only authentic means at our command for getting at the significance of our everyday experiences of the world in which we live.... Consequently, whatever the level of experience, we have no choice but either to operate in accord with the pattern it provides or else to neglect the place of intelligence in the development and control of a living and moving experience. (p. 88)

Pragmatism provides the philosophical framework for the transaction position. In Dewey's pragmatism intelligence is developed through the individual's interaction with the social environment, particularly through solving problems.

In Dewey's conception of problem solving, the first step involves a problematic situation that causes confusion or puzzlement that the individual must resolve. In the second step, the person must define exactly what the problem is. The third step, clarification of the problem, consists of a careful examination or analysis of the factors contributing to the problem. In the fourth step, the person develops hypotheses or "if-then" statements that offer possible solutions to the difficulty; here the person may also generate alternative solutions and consider the possible consequences of each alternative. In the fifth and final step, the person selects one hypothesis or alternative and implements it. If the chosen alternative is successful the person continues his or her activity; if the hypothesis does not work out the individual selects another alternative.

In school, students can apply this methodology in solving the variety of personal and social dilemmas with which they are presented. Dewey argued that, instead of organizing school around traditional subjects, topics should be problem-centered. With his focus on problem solving, Dewey laid the theoretical groundwork for many inquiry approaches in curriculum.

In psychology, Lawrence Kohlberg (1972) claimed that cognitive, developmental psychology was congruent with Dewey's thought. Kohlberg and Mayer argued that "Piaget and Dewey claim that mature thought emerges through a process of development that is ... a reorganization of psychological structures resulting from organism–environment interactions" (p. 456). Gutek (1974) uses the word *transactive* in describing Dewey's philosophy of education since the notion of interaction is so fundamental to this conception of learning.

Finally, liberal economic theory, as articulated by Keynes and Galbraith, represents the social-economic view of the transaction position. Unlike the laissez-faire position, which posits that the marketplace is better left alone, both pragmatism and liberalism embody an optimistic view that people can improve the social environment through rational intervention, and both encourage active efforts toward reform. Related to this is the positive attitude in both pragmatism and liberalism to social planning; both support the view that social planning can improve the overall welfare of society. However, despite this overall support for government involvement in the economy, pragmatists such as Sidney Hook insist on the importance of individual rights within the political structure. In other words, they believe that economic development must take place in a framework of political freedom wherein civil rights are respected. Finally, pragmatic liberalism is committed to the democratic process as a method for developing policy. In Kaplan's (1961) words, "The method is the application of intelligence to social problems." Pragmatic liberalism insists that rational intelligence in the form of the scientific method can resolve most problems and that education plays a key role in developing this rational intelligence.

In education the transaction position can be characterized in the following diagram:

The transaction position can be characterized by emphasis on dialogue between teacher and student. However, this dialogue stresses cognitive interactions in that analysis is stressed more than synthesis and thinking more than feeling. Teaching models which are based in the transaction position include Thelen's Group Investigation Approach, Massialas's Social Inquiry model, Schwab's Scientific Inquiry approach, and Ausubel's Advance Organizer model (Joyce & Weil, 1980). Again, many of these models, particularly those developed by Thelen, Massialas, and Schwab, have their roots in Dewey's conception of inquiry and the scientific method. Much of the curriculum reform in the 1960s was transactional in nature as the new curricula focused on forms of inquiry within various disciplines such as science and social studies.

The transaction position views the learner as rational and capable of intelligent behavior. The student is seen as a problem solver. What is missing in the transaction position is imagination, intuition, and most importantly a sense of the sacred. With regard to the imagination, Sullivan (1977) writes: "There is something lacking in all the conceptual elegance of both Piaget's and Kohlberg's structuralisms. One significant gap is in the area of the 'aesthetic imagination' and the potential role it may play in the development of intellectual and moral understanding" (p. 23). A sense of the sacred, which we find, for example, in native people's spirituality, is also missing in Dewey and in the transaction position. With the stress on the scientific method we are still left with instrumental reasoning, rather than following our deeper intuitions and spiritual insights.

Transformation Position

In the transformation position the universe is seen as an interconnected whole.

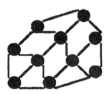

Ecology and subatomic physics has shown that at the heart of nature is the interconnected web. If one part of the whole is affected, there will be changes in the whole organism/system. Perhaps the key distinction between the transformation position and the two previous positions is that the transmission and transaction positions are rooted in dualism. Subject and the object are seen separately. Subatomic physics has shown that the observer affects what he or she is viewing, so in the transformation position the dualism of subject/object is replaced by mutuality and connectedness. Thomas Merton (1975) described this connectedness when he was speaking to people from different faiths at a conference in Calcutta:

> And the deepest level of communication is not communication, but communion. It is wordless. It is beyond words, and it is beyond speech, and it is beyond concept. Not that we discover a new unity. We discover an older unity. My dear brothers, and sisters, we are already one. But we imagine that we are not. And what we have to recover is our original unity. What we have to be is what we are. (p. 308)

The transformation position is rooted in the perennial philosophy (Huxley, 1940). This philosophy focuses on the following themes:

- The interconnectedness of reality and the fundamental unity of the universe

- The intimate connection between the individual's inner or higher self and this unity

- The cultivation of intuition and insight through contemplation and meditation in order to "see" this unity more clearly

- The realization of this unity among human beings leads to social action designed to counter injustice and human suffering

I have already discussed briefly the first theme. The second theme is based on the notion that within each person lies the "divine spark." Christ referred to this spark as "the Kingdom of God within," while the Hindus call it the Atman; this place is also referred to as the Self. When we reside in the Self, we feel in harmony with our environment and at home in the universe. Einstein asked a fundamental question when he said: "Is the universe friendly?" The Self intuitively knows that the universe is friendly while our ego sees the universe as separate and alien, thus, seeks to control and manipulate what it sees as a threat to its existence.

We can realize the Self through various forms of spiritual practice. This third theme of the perennial philosophy often focuses on various forms of contemplative practice. In contemplation or meditation we silently witness the thought system of the ego through the clear awareness of the Self. Through this process there is an awakening to the Self and our connection to the unity (e.g., the Tao, God, or the Brahman). Gandhi (1980) said; "It [silence] has now become a physical and spiritual necessity for me.... After ... I had practised it for some time, I saw the spiritual value of it. It suddenly flashed across my mind that that was the time when I could best hold communion with God" (p. 101).

By deepening our connection to the Self and to the cosmos we feel a basic connection to all life. Gandhi (1980) said: "I believe in the absolute oneness of God, and therefore, of humanity. What though we have many bodies? We have but one soul. The rays of the sun are through refraction. But they have the same source. I cannot therefore, detach myself from the wickedest should nor may I be denied identity with the most virtuous" (p. 72). Because of our fundamental connection to human beings and other forms of life, we are concerned about injustice and suffering. The fourth theme of the perennial philosophy, then, is conscious social action to deal with injustice and suffering.

The social-economic context for the transformation position is emerging. This vision has been articulated by individuals such as Sale (1980), who calls for human scale communities and organization, rather than the gargantuan corporations which cannot respond to local needs and concerns. Recently, Rifkin (1991) has argued that we are moving from geopolitics to biosphere politics which is dedicated to preserving, enhancing, and resacralizing life within the biosphere. Here, the bioregion which is ecologically integrated, will replace the nation-state as the functional unit. Simultaneously, there is developing a greater global consciousness.

Psychologically, the transformation position is rooted in humanistic and particularly in transpersonal psychology. While the transmission psychology focuses on behavior, and the transaction psychology centers on mental processes, transformational psychology recognizes human wholeness, including the aesthetic and spiritual dimensions which are dismissed in the other two conceptions. The work of psychologists such as Rogers (1980), Maslow (1971), and Wilber (1980) have provided a much broader vision of human development.

Transformational education reflects this emphasis on wholeness and connectedness. Here, the curriculum is seen as interconnected with one another:

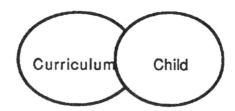

There have tended to be two strands to this position. One strand has focused on the individual. At the extreme, this focus is found in Summerhill (1960), where its founder A.S. Neill felt that the school must fit the child rather than making the child fit the school. Certain elements of the progressive education and humanistic education in the 1960s are also part of this strand. The other strand involves social change orientation, which argues that educators must take a more critical view of the role of schools in society so that schools do not just mirror dominant economic interests, and that schools must be on the cutting edge of social and political change. Today, the work of educators such as Michael Apple and Henry Giroux reflect this orientation. This position is most successful when the two strands are brought together. Certain forms of holistic education attempt to do this.

The Orientations and Holistic Education

When I first started working with the positions, I saw them as separate and unrelated. For example they were seen as three separate circles.

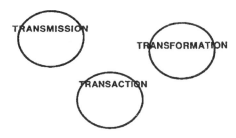

As I began sharing these positions with others and through my involvement in holistic education, I became more concerned about how the positions relate to one another. If everything is at some level connected, then these positions must relate at some level. For example, some people have suggested that the positions are related in a developmental hierarchy similar to Wilber's view.

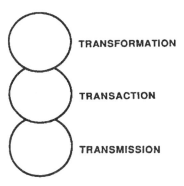

In Wilber's view each level *includes and then transcends* the other level. Thus, the transaction includes transmission, and transformation includes transaction and transmission. There is descriptive validity in this view, but pragmatically in my work with teachers I have found that hierarchies are dysfunctional in that they promote guilt for people who are labelled at the lower levels, and elitism for those who see themselves at the top. It is also interesting to reflect on viewing the nature in terms of a ladder or a circle. Matthew Fox has compared the ladder and circle and has found that the ladder reinforces competition, separateness, and judging; conversely, the circle promotes cooperation, connectedness, and non-judging. (Table is from Fox, 1979, p. 45.)

Ladder	Circle
Up/down	In/out
Flat Earth	Global village
Climbing	Dancing, celebrating
Sisyphian	Satisfying
Competition	Shared ecstasies
Restrictive, elitist: Survival of the fittest	Welcoming, non-elitist: Survival of all
Hierarchical	Democratic
Violent	Strong and gentle
Sky-oriented	Earth-oriented
Ruthlessly independent	Interdependent
Jealous and judgment-oriented	Pride-producing and non-judgmental
Abstract, distance-making	Nurturing and sensual
Linear, ladder-like	Curved, circle-like
Theistic (immanent or transcendent)	Pantheistic (transparent)
Love of neighbor is separate from love of what is at the top	Love of neighbor is love of God

I am more comfortable describing the relationships as connected circles (See following page). One view is to see the relationship as concentric circles and another is nested circles since there are some aspects of the transmission and transaction position that we may not want to include in our vision of holistic education.

It should be clear by now that there are multiple ways that we can diagram or describe the relationship among the positions in relation to holistic education. My students have come up with many other intriguing conceptions beyond what I have presented here. I encourage individuals to see the three orientations as *metaphors that they can play with*. This lets our notion of holistic education change and evolve.

The principal distinguishing factor between holistic education and other forms of education is that holistic education is non-dualistic. *Holistic education, then, is not child-centered but child-connecting.* Through holistic education the child is connected to knowledge,

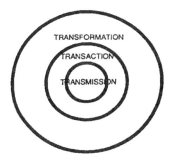 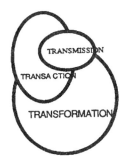

community, the environment, and to the cosmos. This means that we need schools and programs that are based on connectedness and unity rather than fragmentation. In several other contexts I have described what these programs might look like (Miller, [1988] and Miller & Drake, [1990]). However, holistic education must rest to a large degree on the wholeness, or loving consciousness of the teacher, since holistic education can never be reduced to a curriculum or a set of teaching strategies. Holistic teachers will be receptive to what Marsha Sinetar (1991) calls the 21st century mind. Sinetar describes the traditional mind as one which is dualistic, egocentric, focuses on detail, tends to polarize and separate and is fear-motivated. In contrast, the 21st century mind is non-dualistic, integrative, focuses on the whole, resolves paradoxes, and is motivated by love. We will need teachers like the one described by Tagore (1917):

> He had his inspiration not through the medium of books, but through the direct communication of his sensitive mind with the world. The seasons had upon him the same effect as they had upon the plants. He seemed to feel in his blood the unseen messages of nature that are always travelling through space, floating in the air, shimmering in the sky, tingling in the roots of the grass under the earth. The literature that he studied had not the least smell of the library about it. He had the power to see ideas before him as he could see his friends with all the distinctness of form and subtlety of life. (p. 172)

The teacher described by Tagore is one who is rooted in the flow of the universe, the Tao, and from this rootedness comes compassion, wisdom, and sensitivity. The Tao is another name for the nonvisible world which is also called God, (Christianity), the realm of ideas (Plato), emptiness (Buddhism), or the Implicate Order (physicist David Bohm). How does one become rooted in the nonvisible world? This involves a gradual awakening which is often facilitated by various forms of spiritual practice such as meditation and service to others.

In the courses that I teach at OISE I require my students to meditate; to date over 160 students have been through the process. It is beyond the scope of this paper to describe this process, but perhaps I could simply quote the experience of one student's meditation.

> The session began with many thoughts and physical sensations which quickly settled down, and although they didn't totally disappear, were not much in my awareness afterward. It was a very quiet and uneventful meditation with the mantra barely present. In fact, there was not much present at all except the awareness of my self just being there. This continued until towards the end of the session when I began to have certain feelings or knowledge; it's hard to explain how the two combine into one. It's like you know something with every cell of your body, to the point that you actually feel it everywhere. ... I was keenly aware that I was part of all that was around me. There was no distinction between my inner self, my body, and my surroundings. This awareness extended out so that I felt a part of all that there is. As I read what I'm writing, the words sound quite grandiose, whereas the experience was very simple. However, it was also profound, peaceful, and fulfilling at all levels: physical, intellectual, and spiritual.

Out of our spiritual practice we become true resources to our students. If we sense a deep connectedness to the universe, then our students will come in contact with this presence that will support and nourish their own sense of connectedness.

References

Barrett, W. (1979). *The illusion of technique*. New York: Anchor.

Dewey, J. (1969). *Experience and education*. New York: Macmillan Collier Boos. (Originally published in 1938).

Fox, M. (1979). *A spirituality named compassion and the healing of the global village, humpty dumpty and us*. Minneapolis: Winston.

Friedman, M. (1962). *Capitalism and freedom*. Chicago: University of Chicago Press.

Fullan, M. (1991). *The meaning of educational change*. Toronto: OISE Press.

Gandhi, M. (1980). *All men are brothers: Autobiographical reflections*. Krishna Kripalani (Ed.), New York: Continuum.

Gutek, G. L. (1974). *Philosophical alternatives in education*. Columbus: Merrill.

Heilbroner, R. L. (1980). *The worldly philosophers*. New York: Touchstone.

Huxley, A. (1970). *The perennial philosophy*. New York: Harper and Row.

Joyce, B., & Weil, M. (1980). *Models of teaching*. Englewood Cliffs, NJ: Prentice Hall.

Kaplan, A. (1961). *The new world of philosophy*. New York: Random House.

Kent, P. S. (1991). *Instructional and assessment strategies in law: A holistic approach*. Unpublished paper.

Kohlberg, L. N., & Mayer, R. (1972) Development as an aim of education. *Harvard Educational Review, 42,* 449–496.

Maslow, A. (1971). *The farther reaches of human nature.* New York: Viking.

Merton, T. (1975). *The Asian journal of Thomas Merton.* New York: New Directions.

Miller, J. (1983). *The educational spectrum.* New York: Longman.

Miller, J. (1988). *The holistic curriculum.* Toronto: OISE Press.

Miller, J. (in press). Contemplation in higher education: An experiment in teacher development. *Journal of Humanistic Psychology.*

Miller, J., & Seller, W. (1985). *Curriculum: Perspectives and practice.* New York: Longman.

Miller, J., & Drake, S. (1990). Implementing a holistic curriculum. *Holistic Education Review, 3,* 27–30.

Neil, A. S. (1960). *Summerhill: A radical approach to child rearing.* New York: Hart.

Rifkin, J. (1991). *Biosphere politics.* New York: Crown.

Rogers, C. (1980). *A way of being.* Boston: Houghton Mifflin.

Sale, K. (1980). *Human scale.* New York: Perigee.

Sinetar, M. (1991). *Developing a 21st century mind.* New York: Villard.

Sullivan, E. (1977). *Kohlberg's structuralism: A critical appraisal.* Toronto: OISE Press.

Tagore, R. (1917). *My personality.* New York: Macmillan.

Thorndike, E. D. (1913). *Education psychology.* (Vols. 1–3), New York: Teachers College Press.

Wilber, K. (1980). *The atman project.* Wheaton, IL: Theosophical Publishing House.

Chapter 4

Holistic Education in a Prophetic Voice

David Purpel

It is important to distinguish between descriptive and normative analysis of education in that the former seeks to characterize what actually constitutes education activity while the latter seeks to argue which educational activities are more valid, legitimate, and appropriate. When we speak of holistic education in the descriptive sense we are probably referring to the sensible notion that we must attend to and take seriously the whole realm of human learning. In this sense, holistic education serves as a heuristic and corrective force, reminding us of the dangers of the distortions that emerge from overdeterminism on the one hand and neglect on the other. Holistic educators tend to perform an extremely valuable function by concentrating on those dimensions of education commonly neglected or abused by mainstream educators and educational reformers, more particularly such neglected dimensions as concern for intuition, personal knowledge, spiritual reflections, and untapped human potential.[1]

There does not seem to be consensus, however, within the holistic education movement whether this concern is primarily a corrective strategy (designed to provide a more balanced dialogue on education by adding important dimensions to it) or whether it represents primarily a more normative discourse (one in which the argument is that concern for the personal, intuitive, and spiritual is more valuable and appropriate). Of course, there are probably elements of both discourses in the work of holistic educators, but the distinction is important because it raises the question of what ultimate criteria and what conceptual framework are being used to determine notions of valid education. To do so is to immediately invoke those moral, political, and social assumptions that inevitably connect with matters of educational policy and practice. There can be no educational policy or practice independent of a social and cultural context and therefore there is no such theory as "objective" educational theory. The educative process is, for better or worse, inevitably and intimately interrelated with the historic, cultural, normative, political, and economic dimensions of particular communities.

When holistic educators argue that education must be "whole" and that it can be complete only if educators attend not just to the external social and cultural context but also to the inner world of the self and the broader context of the universe, they are both affirming and correcting for a particular socially, culturally, and historically grounded educational analysis. When holistic educators argue instead that "true education" consists of concentrating primarily on the development of personal and spiritual processes that might enable us to transcend our historical, social, and cultural contexts, they are speaking more to a particular affirmation, i.e., of the overriding importance of nourishing a consciousness that might be called more spiritual or mystical. It is one thing to say that humans do not learn by intellect alone or to say that humans are not only social beings — they are also sentient beings. However, it is quite another thing to say that our daily life is basically transient, and that it distracts us from the ultimate meaning that derives from union with the cosmos. In a word, the difference is linked to how much importance we place on the dialectic between culture and the individual and how much importance we place on the individual's connection to the universe.

The holistic education movement's contribution includes raising awareness of the neglect of the person/spiritual/subjective dimensions of education for both mainstream and critical discourses. Conventional educational discourse is of course deeply rooted in the language of technology, positivistic epistemology, and in the values of competition and socio-economic advancement. Much of the educational theory of dissent has provided very powerful critiques of mainstream education primarily on grounds that it has perpetuated social and cultural inequality, oppression, and hegemony. As acute and liberating as this critical discourse has been, it has so far been unable to successfully integrate its analysis with serious concern for the spiritual and subjective dimensions of human existence. This paper attempts to address this issue by arguing that the concern for justice and freedom has been informed by a religious sensibility and, furthermore, that there is an important place for the religious concourse in the project of creating an education that is directed to promoting peace, justice, freedom, and joy.

In this paper I argue for the signal importance of an educational process directed at creating a just society and a compassionate culture. My hope is that this analysis responds to the human impulse for a number of powerful, basic, and to some extent conflicting impulses: autonomy, freedom, equality, justice, community, and fulfillment. Indeed, it is my position that a just and compassionate society is an absolute necessity even if it may not be an absolutely sufficient condition for a life of ultimate meaning. I also wish to emphasize that I do not at all intend in this formulation to claim that education is only or primarily about the process of creating a just society. Educational processes involve an incredible range of activities that include acculturation, socialization, training, initiation, as well as the promotion of inquiry and creativity. Important teaching and learning goes on in a great number of sites — within the individual, in families, on the street, before movie and television screens, in schools and universities, in factories, businesses, and offices, etc. My orientation represents both historical and moral dimensions — historical in that I view my educational concerns as emerging from the historical contingencies of the moment. Further, I believe that educators in this particular historical moment have a special responsibility to ground their policies and programs in a moral vision, i.e., in a conception of what a good society might be.

The Human Narrative

It seems to be in the nature of human beings to sort out and attempt to make meaning out of our activities, and it is quite clear that this process has produced enormously diverse accounts, narratives, histories, and interpretations. These narratives are more than just interesting and intriguing, for they also help to shape communal and individual consciousness; they provide us with meaning and hence with direction, purpose, and energy.

This paper is written within the tradition of those particular narratives that speak to the human struggle to create more just, compassionate, and peaceful communities. The story of these efforts cuts across time and space and speaks to what is most sublime and also to what is most demonic in human possibility. It is not very difficult to see humans as "animals," i.e., being driven by the absolute desire to survive and to satisfy basic needs and gratification. There is ample evidence that humans are capable of doing virtually anything however violent, cruel, and callous in order to satisfy their fundamental needs. What must be remembered, however, is that we live in a culture that has created concepts called "cruelty," "violence," and "callousness," as well as terms like "compassionate," "caring," and "justice." What is extraordinary (if not miraculous) is not that humans like other species are driven towards survival and self-gratification, but unlike other species they also struggle to transcend the limitations of such a consciousness. Although it is problemmatic to say "all," we can surely say that most cultures and societies create limits on what is considered acceptable and unacceptable conduct and behavior; i.e., cultures develop an ethos or spirit of community that serves as a mechanism to control, inspire, and guide its members. Durkheim has described this process as an integration of the personal and social as being grounded in moral and religious frameworks.

> Morality begins with membership of a group.... First, we shall show how society is good and desirable for the individual who cannot exist without it or deny it without denying himself [sic], and how, at the same time, because society suppresses the individual, he cannot desire it without to a certain extent violating his nature as an individual. Secondly, we shall show that society, while being good, constitutes a moral authority.... It is impossible to imagine on the evidence, that morality should serve its unbroken association with religion without ceasing to be itself.... Morality would not longer be morality if it had no elements of religion.... (As quoted in Nisbet, pp. 194–196, 197)

The history of these efforts to build moral communities reflects the incredible paradox, diversity, contributions, and mysteries of the human condition. It is a history of slavery and emancipation; of oppression and democracy; of the invention of napalm and penicillin; the Ku Klux Klan and the Red Cross; and it has produced villains, heroes, demons, and angels. Hilter *and* Gandhi — Louis XIV *and* Thomas Paine — Mother Teresa *and* Henrich Himmler — Joseph

Mengele *and* Madame Curie — the Peace Corps *and* the Hilter Youth. It is also clear that the notion of civilization making steady and continuous progress toward the achievement of a more just, peaceful, and loving world is a serious distortion of reality. Although there is much evidence that many societies have made gains and positive changes in consciousness — e.g., slavery has been abolished in most of the world — there is the harsh and profound reality that even these gains may be overshadowed by significant regression in other spheres. There is evidence that over 100 million people have been killed in wars since 1700, 90% of them in the 20th Century. It is estimated that 2 billion people live in extreme poverty, 450 million suffer from hunger and malnutrition, that 2 in 5 children in American live in poverty, and that there are upwards of 1 million homeless in America. It is surely easy enough to be disheartened by such findings and to be discouraged by the attendant cynicism, apathy, and sense of powerlessness. A consciousness of impotence and cynicism of course compounds and aggravates the enormous pain and suffering that is the consequence of a consciousness of greed, oppression, and callousness. We face catastrophe from the combined forces of evil and apathy, of the dual corruption of power and powerlessness, and from the twin dangers of the affirmation of individual power and the collapse of communal authority.

There are surely new and extremely important dimensions to our present crises — the most paramount of which are the extremely serious risks to the survival of the planet, though it is certainly not news that the human community faces serious crises from a combination of external threats and the collapse of the moral order. We are, however, not without valuable resources in responding to such calls and indeed it is extremely valuable and helpful in such times to reaffirm our most cherished traditions, hopes, dreams, and convictions. A major element in our tradition can be described as a dialectic between affirmation and criticism or, perhaps to use a less linear image, a continuous spiral of criticism and hope: expectations followed by criticism followed by renewed hope and possibility. We have learned not only to dream beyond the narrow limits of human survival and callousness but also to be wary of sentimentality as well as certainty and to be on guard against the violations of our dreams. In the human exploration of our souls, we have discovered a variety of capacities that complicate the struggle for justice — including those of personal deception, denial, evasion, and rationalization. As an antidote to these tendencies, we have come to accept the absolute necessity for maintaining a critical consciousness, a spirit of skepticism, inquisitiveness, and reflectiveness. Indeed, this critical tradition has become so strong and so integral to our culture that it has developed its own set of problematics. Chief among these is to nurture a position of detachment and distance in which a great deal of energy is applied to the analysis and interpretation of ideas, policies, practices with but little, if any, of that energy directed at affirmation. Such a posture can and has generated not only useful insights and understandings, but it has also produced a high degree of moral relativity, political apathy, and cultural cynicism.

The critical traditions that I wish to affirm are ones in which criticism is set as part of a wider and deeper vision. In such traditions, criticism is not an end in and of itself, but a powerful tool in the service of larger moral, cultural, and spiritual aspirations. In such traditions, criticisms are rooted in positive and affirmative commitments that indeed provide the very bases of critique. They are logical consequences of affirmation in that they provide a model and the criteria for making judgments, the heart of the critical enterprise. There can be no criticism without judgment, however implicit and guarded, notwithstanding claims of objectivity and neutrality. Unfortunately, our culture has been able to reify and reduce a critical consciousness through such concepts as "critical thinking" and "objective analysis." This process has the effect of removing (however artifically) technique from judgment and of eliminating the basis and framework within which the critical dimension has been embedded. It is another tragic instance of alienation, in which the meaning-making impulses are actually removed from so-called skills and techniques.

A cornerstone of the larger moral orientation I am discussing is the brilliant Western tradition of critical rationality as reflected in the notion of the Socratic techniques. However, I wish to extend this notion beyond mere technique to its deeper groundings. When I speak of the Socratic tradition, I have particular reference to the Socrates of the *Apology* in which Socrates attempts to describe the meaning of his life and death. In this account we witness the indictment, trial, conviction, and execution of Socrates as well as the justification of his work and his martyrdom. Socrates had been accused of threatening the security of the state by undermining the beliefs of its youth and Socrates indeed admits raising troublesome questions that reveal the shallowness and inadequacies of conventional beliefs. The work is a pivotal part of the narrative of Western

Civilization since it speaks so eloquently and poignantly to the human passion for freedom and truth in the face of the forces of conformity and expediency. Socrates is rightfully one of our major heroes, for he not only exemplifies brilliant intellectuality but also enormous wisdom, courage, and dignity. The images of the shrewd, elderly Socrates calmly taking on his tormentors with consummate wisdom and insight energizes us to maintain faith in the power of the mind and the authority of knowledge. The Greek legacy (as embodied in Socrates) includes the enormous power of the inquiring, incisive, skeptical mind to illumine and extend our vision. It is a legacy that has revolutionized the world and one that, though having its own serious problemmatics, is surely indispensable.

However, there is an extremely important dimension of Socrates's story as told in the *Apology* that is often neglected if not forgotten. I refer to those passages in which Socrates makes it very clear that he is on a spiritual journey and indeed insists that his intellectual engagement with the citizen of Athens is intimately connected to that journey. Socrates is convinced that his search for greater clarity and understanding is sanctioned and required by the gods and thus his queries, reflections, and debates represent sacred responsibilities and obligations. In fact, he makes no separation between church and state, religious and secular, spiritual and humanistic, since a life of meaning is one in which all these elements are in harmony. Shades of holistic education!

The point is that the so-called Socratic Method is not a method or technique at all; it is not about scoring intellectual triumphs or about making debating points. Socrates was indeed pursuing religious fulfillment by carefully examining conventional religious and social ideas intellectually, analytically, and critically not to debunk and deconstruct them but to enrich and deepen them. In responding to his indictment, Socrates has this to say:

> Gentlemen of the jury, I am grateful and I am your friend, but I will obey the gods rather than you and as long as I draw breath and am able I shall not cease to practice philosophy.... Be sure this is what the gods order me to do, and I think there is no greater blessing for the city than my service to the god. For I go around doing nothing but persuading both young and old among you not to care for your body or your wealth in preference to or as strongly as for the best possible state of your soul....

I confess to not knowing very much about the particular nature of Socrates's spiritual consciousness or of the specifics of the religious beliefs of his contemporaries. What is vital for purposes of this analysis is the paradigmmatic power of an orientation in which keen intellectuality is integrally and symbiotically related to a spiritual and moral vision. This relationship has even more particular relevance for us in the discourse of the Biblical prophets, whose narratives contain some of the most central themes of Western morality and spirituality. It is a story with images of slavery and the promise of liberation; of human striving to create communities grounded in a higher law; and of profound commitments to creating a life of piety, justice, compassion, and spiritual salvation.

This paper, to be more precise, therefore is grounded in a particular metaphor of an affirmative, critical tradition, namely in the metaphor of social prophecy. I wish to emphasize that although this concept has deep and vital roots in the Bible, the clear intention is to employ it metaphorically, recognizing that the consciousness and historic dimension of our time and place are extraordinary different from those depicted in the Scriptures. It is also important at the same time to note that in using this metaphor, my intent is to avoid significant distortion of the textual sources but, by the same token, I accept the responsibility to provide (one hopes) a persuasive and creative interpretation.

The point here is not Biblical exegesis but rather to indicate some of the broad but profound influences that some Biblical narratives have had on our consciousness. We can and do interpret great and enduring texts in a variety of ways and indeed it is our human responsibility and destiny to do so. I associate myself with the tradition that sees within the Biblical (as well as other) narratives elements of a profound search for ultimate meaning and a life of justice, peace, and joy. A key part of this narrative is reflected in the accounts described in *Exodus* in which an enslaved people (the Hebrews) are oppressed both by powerful external and brutal forces (Egypt) and by their own sense of powerlessness and despair. The issue of their liberation is linked to the people's capacity to imagine (and hence make possible) transcending their powerfully palpable limits. The prophetic voice (represented here in the figure of Moses) is one which speaks critically, candidly, and boldly. In this case Moses himself has to struggle to accept the vision and to agree to confront the Hebrews with their refusal to fully acknowledge their slavery, and more importantly to recognize the human misery going on in the midst of luxury and splendor as indefensible and unnecessary. In addition, the prophetic voice speaks to hope and possibility by invoking higher forces and principles though the development of a higher consciousness. It becomes Moses's task therefore to teach the Hebrews not only that they are oppressed but they need not and must not be. Furthermore, it is his task to exhort them to have faith in the power of the Divine to infuse the people with the material, spiritual, and moral energy required to break the physical and psychological bonds of physical oppression and personal despair.

Moses, like subsequent prophets, commits himself to the extraordinarily complex, difficult, and frustrating task of raising the consciousness of the oppressed, confronting the power of the oppressors, and dealing with self-doubt, fear, divisiveness, and failures. Moses's early reluctance, his own slow awakening, and his inadequacies as a leader reveal the prophet as human, fallible, vulnerable, and believable while the apparent capacity that Moses had to be in touch with the Divine and to experience and witness the transcendent marks prophets as people who have dramatically extended the range of human possibility. The image of Moses (presumably the most evolved of the most evolved people) at the peak of Mount Sinai is a very powerful metaphor for human transcendence — the possibility of humans reaching for the heavens and of an intimate relationship between God and humanity. What Sinai also represents is the extension of liberation as flight from bondage to liberation as the quest for a community grounded in a vision of ultimate meaning — a shift from freedom defined negatively to a more positive conception of freedom. The covenant represents a commitment to deeply affirm a vision of justice, honor, and piety, and to diligently press for its realization.

This basic pattern of critique, outrage, exhortation, hope, possibility, and vision (what has been called the prophetic voice) recurs not only in other religious narratives but in other social texts as well as in historical events across time and space. In the more literal sense Biblical prophets are clearly identified within the text (e.g., Hosea, Amos, Isaiah, Jeremiah) and each take on the role of alert, inquiring, outraged social critic offering both condemnation of violation of the Covenant and the possibility of redemption through the community's reaffirmation of its commitments. This is very much the configuration of the life of Jesus who severely castigates the community for not only violating the spirit of the Covenant but also for profaning it. Beyond his outrage and indignation he provides a message of renewed hope for transcendence though a consciousness of love, humility, and reaffirmation.

This is not to say Judaism and Christianity are to be equated with the prophetic tradition but only to note that the prophetic tradition remains a vital and powerful force for those committed to a world of justice and peace. This tradition also helps us consider the role of religion in social criticism. Robert Ackerman has argued that the critical function is the very essence of religion, i.e., that it is the responsibility of religion to be alert to the society's reluctance and failure to meet its deepest commitments and to become a voice of protest (e.g., as in *Protest*antism) and renewal.

> Religion ... always retains the potential of developing a pungent social critique, no matter how accommodating a form they have assumed.... Critique does not exhaust religion, but religion that cannot critique is already dead.... What is being suggested here is that the core of religion is potentially critical rather than functional or accommodating. (Ackerman, pp. ix and 24)

It is important to add a note of caution at this point in regard to the problematics and limitations of the metaphor of "prophetic voice." For instance, there is the danger of becoming captured by particular interpretations, as it must be recognized that there have been and continue to be serious controversies regarding biblical interpretation, including those concerning the role and function of the prophets. Furthermore, even if there were a consensus on this, it is also clear that it is dangerous to make direct parallels between and among the social and cultural milieux involved. That was then and this is now, nothwithstanding the reality that the "now" contains important dimension of the "then." We certainly have the right to be selective about which traditions to reaffirm and which to reject but we also have to accept responsibility for making choices rather than justifying them on the basis that we are only reminding ourselves of universal and/or eternal truths. Furthermore, although I find the tradition of spirituality and morally grounded social criticism to be extraordinarily resonant with our current cultural and political crises, I do not choose to support other phenomena associated with biblical narratives, e.g., animal sacrifices, slavery, conquest, patriarchy.

Moreover, we cannot ignore the very important sub-category of "false prophet," which of course raises the basic question of the validity of prophetic voices. One can be outraged, critical, and indignant and be "wrong," i.e., criticality by itself does not guarantee wisdom or rightness. Ultimately, we search for criteria that validate and generate critical dimensions and whether we do or should do this inductively or deductively is not particularly relevant here. Put another way and more crudely, some prophets are "better" than others and this is not necessarily because their analytical capacities are different but rather because their underlying vision is more or less acceptable. The Grand Inquisitor, Martin Luther King, Cotton Mather, Ayotallah Khomeini, and Mohandas Gandhi can all be called prophets in that they integrated their political and social movements with deeply felt religious commitments. One person's passion can indeed become another person's zealotry. Therefore, we will not want to attend to *the* prophetic voice but to prophetic voices and to search for those that are most resonant with our vision of a just, peaceful, and joyous world.

The prophetic tradition has strong roots and resonance in the American experience, perhaps most clearly seen in our Puritan origins. Indeed, the impact of Puritan culture and society on our present consciousness represents our ambivalence toward a morally and religiously grounded orientation. At best the Puritans contributed the values of the authority of individual consciousness and of a morally based community and at worst left a residue of intolerance, rigidity, and self-righteousness. They apparently were not able to conduct their quest for a more just and equitable society without the certainty that they were God's appointed and chosen agents. Their experience (in one of the great ironies and oddities of American history) actually helped to foster a quite contrary religious tradition, namely that of tolerance, diversity, pluralism, and the separation of church and state. The collapse of the Puritan dream, however, did not mean the end but only the elaboration of an American moral and religious consciousness. To this day, for better or worse, American culture often reflects an explicit moral and/or religious orientation in a whole array of areas — from popular culture to foreign policy and from family life to the arts. Some of this is clearly vulgar and self-righteous as in "God Bless America" and the portrayal of certain nations as evil empires but much of this is grounded in the impulse to create a world of meaning, justice, freedom, and joy.

This impulse is eloquently and powerfully reflected in perhaps our country's most sacred text, the Declaration of Independence. Central to this paradigmmatic statement is the notion that "Governments are instituted among Men [sic], deriving their just Powers from the Consent of the Governed," a political expression of the moral and religious principles that "... all Men are created equal, that they are endowed by their Creator with certain inalienable rights...." The statement goes on to affirm the vital responsibility of the citizenry to maintain patient but critical vigilance of the government's fidelity to those principles since, if the government should become despotic, "it is their Right, it is their Duty to throw off such Government." In an echo of Sinai, an emerging people commits itself to a religious and moral vision as the boundaries of a new nation.

As the author of the Declaration of Independence, it is no surprise that Jefferson saw education as a critical dimension in the creation of the new democratic society. The suspicion of government's capacity to oppress requiring "eternal vigilance" and the basic principle of the "consent of the governed" combine to require an alert, informed, and critical citizenry. Thus education in America shifted from a focus on the training of ministers and the enlightenment of an elite to an essential instrument of the empowerment of the individual and the preservation of the democratic vision. Later John Dewey saw the schools as the "laboratory" for democracy, where students and teachers could experience and reflect upon the problems and difficulties inherent in creating a world based on a commitment to dignity, justice, rationality, and tolerance. George Counts took this one step further by claiming for education the responsibility for teaching the process not only of understanding but transforming society. In a memorable statement evocative of prophetic rhetoric Counts once wrote:

> If the schools are to be really effective, they must become centers for the building, and not merely for the contemplation, of our civilization. This does not mean that we should endeavor to promote particular reforms through the educational system. We should, however, give to our children a vision of the possibilities which lie ahead and endeavor to enlist their loyalties and enthusiasms in the realization of the vision. Also, our social institutions and practices, all of them, should be critically examined in the light of such a vision. (Counts, p. 37)

Education, Society, and Culture in the 1990s

What then are educators who strive to evoke these prophetic traditions to make of our present historical moment? How well are we as a people doing in the struggle to reduce misery, poverty, suffering, oppression and to increase justice, peace, harmony, equality, and joy? We pose these questions not only because they are obviously of enormous import in and of themselves but more particularly because they ought to serve as the major point of departure for educators. Organized education is to be seen not predominately in the service of scholarship nor primarily to serve the state or the economy but primarily to serve the task of nurturing, nourishing, and sustaining the quest to meet our highest aspirations and most profound commitments. The standards of a society and culture (and hence of its educational institutions) involve concerns for the degree of freedom, equality, justice, and fulfillment enjoyed by its members.

The recognition of both the importance of affirming our solid and enduring social and cultural achievements as well as the dangers inherent in profound pessimism does not, however, mitigate the harsh and obscene reality of the horrors of our present condition, worldwide as well as nationally and locally. There are no end of indices, statistics, and observations to demonstrate and evoke the starkness, depth, and extent of profound and unnecessary human suffering. Indeed, this could be demonstrated by a brief exposition of only one of this century's many catastrophes: World War I, Auschwitz, Hiroshima, World War II, Viet Nam, the Sub-Saharan famines, oil spills, the greenhouse effect, Cambodia, et al. It is extraordinary that such a list can only be suggestive and not definitive; there simply is not the space to list all or even most of the truly horrible events of this century.

There have been a great many attempts to explain and provide meaning for such stupefying phenomena in the poignant assumption that there are indeed meaningful explanations. Attendant, then, to this terrible material and physical destructiveness has been a corresponding erosion of the spirit. Alienation, fragmentation, anomie, fear, and loneliness are virtually household names and routines. There is deep thirst for meaning and direction as a consequence of an increasing sense of meaninglessness and existential despair. The society and the schools urge us to work hard, strive for personal success, and compete with ourselves, our colleagues, and our enemies. Some (too many) people respond with drugs, crime, suicide, and depression. The society and schools extol individual achievement and indeed equate it with virtue. Some (surely too many) people respond with divorce, loneliness, and anomie. The society and the schools exhort us to be "number one" and that we are risking our loss of economic and political supremacy. Some (far too many) people respond with racism, sexism, jingoism, and homophobia. The society demands more control, discipline, hard work, and competition and the profession responds with more sophisticated tests and more clever modes of monitoring students and teachers. The people cry out for meaning, wisdom, and deliverance — and the society and school respond fearfully with more control, more jargon, more retrenchment, and less meaning and wisdom than ever.

The response of the dominant professional community has been at best evasive and at worst complicitous. Much of the profession has tried to stake out an area of expertise in which the broader cultural, moral, and social issues are left to nonprofessionals. This so-called professional orientation is one in which educators are cast as resource people charged with researching and implementing policy decisions. In a word, to follow but not to shape orders. The great preponderance of educational research is technical, and indeed the term *research* has been reified and reduced to come to mean experimental, positivistic, quantified investigation. Even the broader cultural, social, and moral issues become objects of study rather than perspectives for affirmation.

A tragic consequence of this narrow, timid, and self-serving professional posture is the appallingly vulgar and ill-informed nature of the public dialogue on educational matters. It is surely true that in the long-run basic educational decisions emerge from a social and cultural consensus rather than from professional expertise. All the more reason, then for the profession to meet its responsibilities to help the public to frame its dialogue in ways consistent with the complexities, paradoxes, and profundities of the fundamental issues. The timidity and irrelevance of the professional response to our crises is pitiful and borders on the criminal. The moral fabric of our culture is in tatters and the public debates how much homework should be assigned. There are hundreds of thousands of people living in the streets; racial polarization increases; children suffer from neglect and malnutrition and educators offer up career ladders, standardized tests, more requirements, and more school time.

Happily, this is surely not to say that such reactions constitute the entire range of professional response. There is indeed a very lively, imaginative, and provocative body of educational criticism and theory that goes far beyond the toadying and myopic quality of the dominant elements of the profession. Much of the critical literature speaks directly and cogently to the cultural, social, and political aspects of education and to the necessity for rooting education reform in social and cultural transformation. The term "critical pedagogy" has been loosely applied to this broad school of educational criticism in reference to its major reliance on neo-Marxist critical theory.[2] Critical pedagogy puts a great deal of reliance on raising the consciousness of people's lived experiences, particularly as they relate to issues of power, freedom, equality, and justice. This school of thought has made and continues to make very important contributions to educational theory and has energized a great number of educators with its message of criticism, hope, and possibility. Unfortunately, it has also met a great deal of resistance and even more unfortunately, it has largely failed to enter the consciousness of mainstream professionals or of the public. There are a number of possible explanations for the failure of these powerful ideas to have more impact (e.g., genuine and profound disagreement, the complexities of the analysis, and language). Many in the critical pedagogy movement are currently working on enriching their theoretical underpinnings through moral and psychological inquiries and broadening their political base by adapting a positive inclusivist approach, by reflecting on how their theory is related to a wide array of marginalized groups.

There are other qualitatively different voices of educational criticism that speak more directly to issues of psychological constriction, spiritual alienation, and ontological sterility. These voices emerge from traditions of progressive and libertarian education that stress the vital importance of individual freedom, creativity, and unfettered human potentiality (Stoddard, 1991). In addition, these voices are often augmented by chords that resonate with New Age themes of spiritual quest, ecological concerns, and cosmological perspectives (LePage, 1991). This broad movement has a major advantage over the critical pedagogy orientation in that its psychological and spiritual perspectives are shared by a great many people, although the lay public for the most part has failed to extend these perspectives into their interpretation of educational policies and practices. However, what these critical voices add by way of their concern for psychological, emotional, and spiritual matters is diminished by their relatively weak efforts to integrate their ideas with the social, political, cultural, and moral dimensions of the human struggle.

Another critical difference between these two very broad schools of educational criticism is found in the extremely vital issue of assumptions regarding human nature. At the real risk of oversimplification, these differences involve degrees of optimism, pessimism, and cynicism. One side is accused of sentimentality, romanticism, and denial while the other is accused of being overwhelmed if not energized by vision of gloom, despair, and futility. This is related in part to theories of change which involve, on the one hand, the view that transformation must emerge from fundamental changes in social, cultural, and economic structures or, on the other hand, that transformation can emerge only from significant changes in human consciousness. While both are clearly needed and are surely interrelated, the rhetoric usually stresses one or the other. Those who stress the predominant importance of cultural and social transformation are likely to see such a process as involving quasi-permanent conflictual and frustrating struggles with uncertain prospects. Many theorists who focus on the psychological and spiritual dimensions are apt to be much more optimistic, if not euphoric, about the possibilities of quantum leaps in consciousness and are therefore able to envision the possibility of attaining significant and dramatic transformation.

To sum up our present section, we see a world at serious risk from a variety of material horrors (famine, disease, oppression, war, pollution) and suffering from a variety of diseases of the spirit (moral numbness, callousness, alienation, and powerlessness). The culture's educational response to these crises tends to promote the forces that contribute to the crises: concern for competition, achievement, hierarchy, and material success. The profession for the most part has renounced its responsibility to provide moral leadership, taking on instead a posture of being detached, technical experts. There are important and vital voices of educational dissent and alternatives, but they are divided particularly in how they view the relative significance of psychological and cultural forces and their degree of optimism.

I believe that the single most powerful contribution that the holistic education movement is making to the field of educational theory is the power of the metaphor of holism, i.e., of being aware of the parts, the sum of the parts, and that which is more than the sum of the parts. Further work is obviously needed to develop a more comprehensive theoretical framework that gives sufficient attention to all the important dimensions of human experience and education. I believe that the prophetic tradition can contribute to the further development of such theoretical work and will in the remainder of this essay sketch out some ideas on what these contributions might be.

My own view is that educational institutions can only be truly transformed by social and cultural pressures. There is no credible evidence that the schools have ever been a major force in cultural and social transformation. At the same time, it is clear that they constitute at least both a force and a resource and it is vital that whatever the degree of their influence that they utilize their valid possibilities optimally. Although it is to the culture that we must ultimately look for the possibilities of transformation, the profession has an extremely important role in facilitating and guiding public dialogue and social movements. Significant experience as practitioners and theorists provide educators with a unique and necessary perspective to interpret the meaning of educational policies and practices in relationship to the culture's most profound aspirations. This responsibility includes not only developing critical and sensitive insights but also the task of making these insights vital and accessible to the general public. This task must seek a balance between the ethical requirements to convey the complexities, paradoxes, contradictions, and sensitivities of the crises with the moral competence to offer genuine and viable possibilities for transformation. I believe that a great deal of the necessary work has already been done by our current educational theorists and visionaries and the hope of this paper is to further the development of a greater degree of consensus among the varying views of these critics.

Education in a Prophetic Voice

In this section, I sketch out an orientation toward education which reflects a selective blending of the voices of educational criticism and vision, an orientation rooted in the sacred and profound traditions which endeavor to speak in a prophetic voice. In addition to being informed by the contributions of these educational critics, I will be relying on the work of Abraham Heschel, Matthew Fox, and Cornel West to enrich and enhance these voices.

These three theologians can all be said to be in the prophetic traditions, although clearly they have very different perspectives and offer their own unique contributions. All three passionately affirm the struggle to ground moral, political, and social struggles in spiritual and transcendental visions. I believe strongly that the work exemplified by these three champions of the "wretched of the earth" has powerful possibilities and implications for educators and those interested in the educative process. Moreover, their work also would seem to provide a nexus between those educational critics now divided by their differences on the significance of social/cultural/political forces as opposed to moral and spiritual ones.

Abraham Joshua Heschel's monumental analysis and interpretation of the biblical prophets rejects the necessity for such dualism. It is the prophets, according to Heschel, who established the profound possibility that humans have "the ability to hold God and man in a single thought." The prophetic consciousness is one in which the material and the spiritual are not separate categories but vital and interacting dimensions of human existence. God is seen by Heschel not as a detached observer eagerly but remotely watching to see how humans are doing; rather the God of the Prophets is a God of pathos and compassion whose own being is intimately linked to human destiny. This God is actively involved in the Covenant with humanity and makes it clear that deviations and violations of the Covenant stir divine anger, grief, and dismay. The prophetic sensibility is one which registers the profundity of the human activities, behaviors, and policies likely to incur this wrath and grief. In this sense, prophets are not to be seen as seers, sorcerers, or crystal ball readers but as shrewd and sensitive social and cultural critics. Their task is to interpret the degree to which the community has been true to its commitments and to speak openly of the serious dangers that will almost surely befall continuing violations of these commitments. Their message is, however, more than warning, outrage, and indictment but also one of hope, possibility, and redemption. What is recognized here is the inevitability of the human propensity to seek advantage rather than justice, as well as the possibility of transcendence over this propensity. This possibility lies in the dialectic between human imagination and divine energy. Social prophesy exists to remind the human community of its responsibilities to engage in the enormously important struggle to create a humane community worthy of divine approval and to renew its commitment to those goals.

Central to this process is the concept of responsibility, or more particularly in Heschel's terms, "the ability to respond to divine commitments and imperatives." This ability involves the capacity to be alert, critical, and active and is absolutely crucial to the struggle for human freedom and fulfillment. The ability to respond is crucial because humans have the capacity to deny freedom to themselves and to others because of their impulse for greed, selfishness, and personal gain. Indeed, in Heschel's terms, "The opposite of freedom is not determinism but hardness of heart." To be free is to be able to enjoy the fruits of life in a just, caring, and compassionate community" (Heschel, 1962, p. 14).

There are other somewhat more subtle barriers to the emergence of such a community besides the propensity to evil, particularly the obstacles created by passivity, despair, and equivocation. Prophets speak with indignity and outrage at both flagrant and insidious violations of the commitment to the poor, hungry, and oppressed, being well aware of the dangers of both evil and indifference. In words evocative of the passion and eloquence of the prophets, Heschel says:

> Above all, the prophets remind us of the moral state of a people: Few are guilty, all are responsible. If we admit that the individual is in some measure conditional or affected by the spirit of society, an individual's crime discloses society's corruption. In a community not indifferent to suffering, uncompromisingly impatient with cruelty and falsehood, continually concerned for God and every man, crime would be infrequent rather than common. (Heschel, 1962, p. 165)

Matthew Fox, writing from a Catholic perspective, echoes the concept of co-creation in which humans participate in the further creation of a world inspired by a will toward justice, love, peace, and joy. His theology reaffirms a cosmological consciousness and insists that we situate our being in the universe lest we commit the error of intellectual shallowness and the ontological arrogance of anthropocentrism, an undue concern for human/worldly perspectives. However, his mysticism does not at all take him into a totally contemplative position but actually quite the reverse. To Fox, the mystical, the divine, the universal, the human, and the social are to be seen in their uniqueness, diversity, and in their totality. Day-to-day life is to reflect and energize a universe of joy, vibrancy, and love in which we dance with the awe and radiance of the mystery (Fox, 1979).

Unlike other so-called New Age figures, Fox speaks directly, cogently, and specifically to social, political, and economic concerns. His passionate devotion to the well-being of the planet is deeply informed by an understanding of how our political and economic system contributes to our ecological dangers. Indeed, he speaks out against the spiritual dangers of a religious detachment in which the spiritual agenda of creating a world of justice and harmony can be ignored. Fox is particularly concerned that we be aware of the distinction between compassion and sentimentality since human compassion is the process of creating a daily life infused with divine light. Compassion involves genuine sharing of pain and joy and is inherently communal and interdependent, while sentimentalism involves detached, shallow, and superficial recognition of the pain and joy of others. Compassion provides an opportunity to affirm and manifest human relationship and commitment while sentimentality facilitates separation and irresponsibility.

The struggle for creating a compassionate community is significantly facilitated through art, or more precisely through what Fox calls "art as meditation." In this concept, art is not limited only to the specially talented, but defined as the human process of imagination, creativity, and meaning making. It is the human genius to play, to dream, to have vision, and to imagine and it is art that gives form to these images, through the creation of rituals, stories, poems, paintings, sculpture, crafts, et al. In turn, these images guide and help us to interpret our lives and to make meaning of them. Clearly this process is critical to our responsibility to share in the creation of the world that is part of a vast and mysterious universe and hence one that must be enriched and nourished. It is to the creative process that we must look for our ability to move beyond the horror of our present existence and to imagine and therefore make possible a more loving, compassionate, and joyful world. When we recognize that we have in fact created a world, we can accept the responsibility and appreciate the possibility of re-creating it.

Cornel West's academic brilliance and astonishing scholarship is powerfully nourished by his affirmation of the Afro-American experience and the traditions of the black church. He proposes a bold and critical synthesis between Marxist analysis and Christian theology with particular attention to the plight of the oppressed and marginalized. His work is a superb blending of prophetic traditions, American pragmatism, and black liberation theology written with eloquence, power, elegance, and authority. He affirms the Christianity that speaks to the poor, the meek, and the oppressed with its promise of ultimate salvation. It is this promise that West believes can enable us to overcome our fears and dread of death, loss, and meaninglessness and thus provoke us with energy to struggle for what he calls "penultimate salvation," the redemption that derives from the struggle to create a just and caring community.

He also affirms American traditions of political protest against tyranny and declarations of independence from the domination of European philosophical traditions. In his book *The American Evasion of Philosophy*, West traces the origins of pragmatism to the optimism, individualism, and idealism of Ralph Waldo Emerson and to his efforts to side-step the distraction of metaphysical speculations. West critically describes and analyzes the contributions of others (such as Dewey, Mills, James, Du Bois, Niebuhr, and Rorty) to this pragmatic tradition and adds his own perspective which he calls "prophetic pragmatism." West approves of the American intellectual propensity to avoid traditional philosophic inquiry:

> [T]he claim is that once one gives up on the search for foundations and the quest for certainty, human inquiry into truth and knowledge shifts to the social and communal circumstances under which persons can communicate and cooperate in the process of acquiring knowledge. What was once epistemological now highlights the values and operations of power requisites for the human production of truth and knowledge.... Prophetic pragmatism makes the political motivation and political substance of the American evasion of philosophy explicit.... The emancipatory social experimentalism that sits at the center of prophetic politics closely resembles the democratic elements of Marxist theory, yet its flexibility shuns any dogmatic, a priori, or monistic pronouncement. (West, 1990)

West, a deeply committed visionary, is no romantic and has internalized the bitter struggle of his community to make even minimal gains and addresses the dialectic between tragedy and progress directly:

> Prophetic pragmatism refuses to side-step this issue. The brutalities and atrocities in human history, the genocidal attempts in this century, and the present-day barbarities require that those who accept the progressive and prophetic designations put forth some conception of the tragic ... yet prophetic pragmatism is a child of Protestant Christianity wedded to left romanticisms.... Prophetic pragmatism ... tempers its utopian impulse with a profound sense of the tragic character of life and history.... Prophetic pragmatism ... confronts candidly individual and collective experiences of evil in individuals and institutions — with little expectation of ridding the world of *all* evil. Yet it is a kind of romanticism in that it holds many experiences of evil to be neither inevitable nor necessary but rather the results of human agency, i.e., choice and actions. (West, 1990, p. 228)

This powerful reaffirmation of the human responsibility to avoid the twin perils of despair and sentimentality provide us with a language that helps in the struggle against contemporary weariness, anomie, and powerlessness. It is to remind us of both the sublimity of our aspirations and the finitude of our endeavors although West is not unaware of the lingering sense of futility and meaninglessness that pervades our era. He chides those afflicted with this malaise for ignoring the redemptive qualities of a religious consciousness: "The severing of ties to churches, synagogues, temples, and mosques by the left intelligentsia is tantamount to political suicide; it turns the pessimism of many self-defeating and self-pitying secular progressive intellectuals into a self-fulfilling prophecy" (West, 1990, p. 234).

The following quotation from West is unsurpassed in its ability to capture the essence of the prophetic tradition and to speak its essence in the context of our present movement. It can serve as a vital credo for the development of an educational process that can inform the struggle for a world of love, justice, peace, and joy. It is a statement that can energizes us with its soaring hopes and its attainable possibilities:

> Human struggle sits at the center of prophetic pragmatism, a struggle guided by a democratic and libertarian vision, sustained by moral courage and existential integrity, and tempered by the recognition of human finitude and frailty. It calls for utopian energies and tragic actions, energies and actions that yield permanent and perennial revolutionary, rebellious, and reformist strategies that oppose the status quo of our day. These strategies are never to become ends in themselves, but rather to remain means through which are channeled moral outrage and human desperation in the face of prevailing forms of evil in human societies and in human lives. Such outrage must never cease, and such desperation will never disappear, yet without revolutionary, rebellious and reformist strategies, credible and effective opposition wanes. Prophetic pragmatism attempts to keep alive the sense of alternative ways of life and of struggle based on the best of the past. In this sense, the praxis of prophetic pragmatism is tragic action with revolutionary intent, usually reformist consequences, and always visionary outlook. (West, 1990, p. 229)

These powerful and eloquent writers remind us of what our work entails rather than provide us with job descriptions. Our work as educators ought to have little to do with increasing productivity, patriotism, and pride but much more to do with meeting our responsibilities to create a compassionate consciousness. Schools should not be objects of detached research and study but subjects of committed search and inquiry. They should be houses of study and affirmation and not sorting and counting houses. An education that speaks in a prophetic voice responds not to the possibility of becoming rich and famous but to the possibility of becoming loving and just. Its reference point is not the possible erosion of America's economic and military might but humanity's real erosion of its vision of universal harmony, peace, and fulfillment. Such an education is not rooted in strategies, planning, curriculum guides, decision plans, or programs for developing human resources but rather in the mystery that enables us to dream and hope beyond our present realities.

This educational vision encompasses the awe and majesty of the universe as well as the extraordinary capacities of humans to make meaning and create cultural and social structures. It is an education that commits itself to recreating human consciousness and structures in order to make real our dreams for justice, harmony, peace, and joy. This commitment involves a deep commitment to the democratic process that enables us to celebrate our freedom, interdependence, and individuality. The commitment also requires us to be alert to its violations and perversions and the necessity to respond to oppression and injustice with outrage and to be determined to engage in the struggle. It is an education whose starting point is not "excellence" or "achievement" but the grotesque realities of an obscene level of unnecessary human suffering. As members of the human community we need to be reminded that we have created hunger, war, poverty, and oppression and as citizens of the universe we must renew our covenant to repair the world. As simultaneous members of the human community and constituents of the universe we can find meaning in the intimate relationship between the pains we have cruelly inflicted and the healing we have lovingly extended.

Such an education links heaven and earth, moral and spiritual consciousness, and society and the individual. It also vitally requires all human energies — the mind, the intellect, the body, the soul, and their unity. It must take into account our history and our traditions of knowing and must seek to benefit from accumulated knowledge and wisdom. Such an education requires the development of the skills of experential and expressive writing; of critical and appreciative reading; knowledge of various symbolic systems; deep understanding of several cultures, languages, and histories; significant understanding of several modes of research; the capacity to create and imagine. It is an education in which knowledge, criticality, and skills are necessary but not sufficient, since such capacities need to be informed by moral energy and enriched by the social and practical skills required of those who would make a world.

What is also required is the courage and determination to maintain the struggle, especially since our education will likely reveal the depth, persistence, and well-nigh intractability of injustice, greed, callousness, and cruelty. We can take solace and comfort from the reality that the task of creating a just world is a relatively new one in the context even of human, never mind geologic, history. Moreover, we must celebrate the majesty of a struggle that binds us to the highest ideals of those who came before us and that will inspire even greater aspirations by those who come after us. As it is written in the Talmud, "The task is not for us to finish, but neither are we free not to take part in it."

References

Ackerman, R. J. (1985). *Religion as critique*, Amherst, MA: University of Massachusetts Press.

Counts, G. (1962). *Education and the foundations of freedom*. Pittsburgh: University of Pittsburgh Press.

Fox, M. (1979). *A spirituality named compassion and the healing of the global village*, Minneapolis: Winston.

Heschel, A. (1962). *The prophets*, 2 Vols. New York: Harper & Row.

LePage, A. (1991). Creation spirituality and the reinventing of education. In R. Miller (Ed.), *New directions in education*. Brandon, VT: Holistic Education Press.

Nisbet, R. (1974). *The sociology of Emile Durkheim*. New York: Oxford University Press.

Plato (1985). *The trial and death of Socrates*. Translated by G.M.A. Grube. Indianapolis: Hacket.

Stoddard, L. (1991). The three dimensions of human greatness: A framework for redesigning education. In R. Miller (Ed.), *New directions in education*. Brandon, VT: Holistic Education Press.

West, C. (1989). *The American evasion of philosophy*, Madison: University of Wisconsin Press.

Notes

1. My major sources for descriptions of the current holistic education movement are two books by Ron Miller: *What are schools for? Holistic education in American culture*, an excellent historical analysis of the movement's roots and current directions; and *New directions in education*, an anthology of articles from *Holistic Education Review*. Among the more articulate theorists in this area are Miller, Phil Gang, Lynn Stoddard, and Edward Clark.

2. Prominent among these writers are Henry Giroux, Michael Apple, Roger Simon, Svi Shapiro, Michelle Fine, and Linda Christian-Smith.

Chapter 5

Critical Theory and Holistic Education: Carrying on the Conversation

Kathleen Kesson

The other night, my son Steve had a dream in which a UFO, radiating blue light, hovered outside his bedroom window. His dream-self instinctively turned to get his camera which was lying on the floor beside his futon. When he turned back to the window, camera in hand to photograph the amazing sight, the phenomena had vanished. In his dream, he stayed up the entire following night, camera in hand, waiting for the UFO to return, so he could capture its image. It never returned. His dream-self knew that it didn't return precisely *because* he waited with camera.

Earlier in the evening, Steve and I had been having a conversation about the difficulty of capturing the essence of subtle subjective experiences and intuitions with familiar language symbols. We had talked about the way in which nuances of meaning often evaporate under the onslaught of words, like the dream-craft avoiding the appropriation of its image.

Engaging in a critical analysis of holism may be somewhat like trying to photograph the UFO of my son's dream. It might be argued that holism constitutes a self-sufficient paradigm, and that to subject it to the focussed lens of a critical discourse is to steal away its substance, to dilute it, negate it, or trivialize it. After all, holism embodies a revolt against the diminution of meaning wrought by an exclusive focus on calculating reason.

Existing within what Wittgenstein would call a "language game" that embraces the ephemeral world of affect, imagination, intuition, fantasy, and dream, holism implies the creation and legitimation of a cultural space for what curriculum theorist James MacDonald has termed the "mytho-poetic" dimension of experience. MacDonald proposed a methodolodgy for understanding that was essentially separate from science (with its practical interest in control) and critical theory (with its practical interest in emancipation). He called this the "mytho-poetic imagination" — the realm of insight, visualization, and imagination — and suggested that its practical interest is meaning. This emergent holistic perspective, according to education theorist Ron Miller,

> dissolves the traditional dichotomies between mind and body, between spirit and matter.... The central tenet of the holistic worldview — and this is the basis for the term *holistic* — is its emphasis on the integration of the inner qualities of human life with the outer physical, social world. (Miller, 1990, p. 59)

Extending its traditional concern with personal human development, holistic educational thought has begun to intermingle questions of subjective meaning with an ideal of social transformation.[1] It thus joins a sizable body of thought which explores the dialectical relationship between the worlds of subjective experience and the social world. Scholars associated with a tradition known as critical theory share this concern for the development of an "authentic self" and its relation to the transformation of the social-cultural world.

Critical theory is a Western Marxist tradition which explores previously neglected aspects of Marxism in light of contemporary events. Despite a certain unity of purpose, critical theory is not a unitary philosophical system, but a diverse tradition of thought identified with two main branches. The first centered around the Institute for Social Research established in Frankfurt, Germany, in 1923. The key figures in this tradition that will be referred to in this essay are Max Horkheimer, Theodor Adorno, and Herbert Marcuse. Another main branch of critical theory has grown up around the more recent work of Jurgen Habermas in philosophy and sociology. The themes investigated by the Frankfurt School were extensive and highlight the wide range of thought of its members: the effects of mass culture on the individual, positivism as a dominant mode of constructing knowledge, family structure and human development, theories of capitalism and the bourgeois state, the analysis and critique of reason, and the effects of science and technology upon culture. In this essay I will explore some interconnections between critical theory and the emergent holistic paradigm, highlight some of the differences, and begin an analysis of holistic education through the framework of a critical theory.

I write from the somewhat uncomfortable position of a friendly critic of holistic thought, informed both by my studies in comparative religion and a quarter century of meditation practice, as well as a graduate education in critical social theory, curriculum theory, and philosophy. While I find great power and generative energy in the contemporary holistic vision, I also discern elements which may contain seeds of future, and as yet little understood forms of domination, as well as elements which might serve to strengthen and sustain the social forms it proposes to transform. I will elaborate on these suppositions later.

I find many holistic thinkers peculiarly unreceptive to an in-depth analysis of issues pertinent to their vision of social transformation. Much holistic writing and discourse is rather global and abstract, and I sense a hesitancy to bring it into more concrete and particular terms. Perhaps this is because we are in something of a "plastic historical moment," in which the old has departed and the new has not yet arrived. In my many conversations with holistic educators, however, I am disturbed by an almost wholesale rejection of critical analysis and a tendency to confuse "critical theory" with either "critical thinking" (usually defined as higher order thinking skills) or an outdated form of scientific Marxism, with its deterministic class analysis. I hope this essay might help to clear up this basic conceptual misunderstanding.

I suspect the rejection of a critical perspective derives from an unrelenting avoidance of conflict that seems to be related to such popular metaphysical themes as "think positively," "create your own reality," "all suffering is in your mind," "visualize peace," and "don't worry, be happy," themes which have almost achieved the status of New Age orthodoxy. I am also troubled with what I perceive as a somewhat vacuous spirituality, which Robert Bellah interprets as a content-free private world of great intensity:

> There is a vehement insistence on selfhood, but it is an absolutely empty self; except for the sheer quantity of excitation there is nothing at all.... Symbolic, ethical, or religious content terms get swallowed up in the language of psychic process. (Bellah, 1981, p. 130)

It is this almost exclusive focus on the "process" and the concomitant renunciation of interest in "content" that I find most worrisome. (This process/content point will be explored in relation to education later). I suspect that this imbalance derives from holism's resuscitation of an almost Hegelian Idealism, which perceives human subjectivity as the primary theater of human experience, and anything real, material or tangible as merely props. Ed Clark, whom I believe represents this point of view, writes,

> Because all human knowledge and experience is, at its most fundamental level, subjective in nature, one's profoundly personal experience of "reality" is the primary filter through which one views and evaluates everything that happens. (Clark, 1991, p. 46)

Clark goes on to suggest that a more complex analysis of knowledge and perception that might take into account the influences of language, culture, and experience on human subjectivity is "behavioristic," a misapprehension which at worst condones a lapse into solipsism, and at the very least will result in the impoverishment of holistic educational theory. This Idealist interpretation also contradicts what Miller (above) sees as the *dissolution* of the traditional dichotomies between mind and body, spirit and matter. While I don't wish to belabor the point, this core assumption pertains to the controversy over what should be the locus of educational transformation — whether the personal consciousness of individuals is the only significant site for change or whether activists also need to be concerned with wider structural changes. David Purpel suggests a dialectical understanding of these aspects of transformation as a way of moving beyond the controversy (Purpel, 1992). I agree, and I strongly believe that holism, both as a social movement and a theoretical perspective, would be enriched by the inclusion of new ideas from the sociology of knowledge, feminist thought, and critical theory — an inclusion which will involve reconceptualizing some of its more archaic metaphysical assumptions.

Critical theory not only shares with holism the critique of techno-industrial-bureaucratic society, it also challenges the dominant epistemologies of the Enlightenment, epitomized by rationality and the scientific method. Unlike many proponents of holism, however, critical theorists do not see the rejection of reason as unproblematic. Critical theorist Herbert Marcuse held that the goals of a critical approach to society are "the emancipation of consciousness, the nurturing of a decentralized political movement and the reconciliation of humanity and nature" (in Held, 1980, p. 224), goals which are mutually consistent with those of holistic thinkers. Marcuse strove to relate the comprehensive picture of human development and the social process offered by critical theory to existent and emergent forms of opposition to the status quo "no matter how fragmented, distorted or hopeless they may seem at the moment" (William Leiss, in Held, p. 224).

Holistic thought, while not necessarily "fragmented, distorted or hopeless," does embrace a chaotic constellation of themes — some might call it a hodgepodge of borrowed ideas.[2] Like critical theory, however, it serves to highlight the gulf between prevailing forms of human existence and unrealized potentialities. Despite significant theoretical differences, both ways of thinking bring into focus wants and desires which reflect a certain frustration with the way things are and a longing for a "different order."

Critical theorists, according to Jeremy Shapiro, have shied away from the possibility of synthesizing individual liberation and radical politics, a neglect which has served to distance its actual practice from its theoretical framework. (I would suggest that critical feminist theory/practice is a significant exception to this thesis). Critical theory has also been accused of "critiquing itself into a corner" and neglecting the development of a dynamic alternative vision for society. Much of its attention has focused upon the complex ways in which social and political forms constitute individual consciousness. Proponents of critical theory

> seek to reveal society for what it is, to unmask its essence and mode of operation, and to lay the foundations for human emancipation through deep-seated social change. (Gibson, Burrell, Gareth, & Morgan, 1979)

Holism, in contrast, is a somewhat amorphous activist movement that tends to be nontheoretical and relatively acritical, but which has an almost magical faith in the cultural transformation that will result when sufficient numbers of people experience a "shift" in consciousness. I believe that both perspectives would benefit from a serious and sustained conversation.

The Emergence of Holistic Thought

In his book, *What Are Schools For?*, Ron Miller documents the evolution of holistic thought in America, suggesting that it is the story of an ongoing conflict between certain core themes of American culture (specifically Protestant Christianity, scientific reductionism, restrained democratic ideology, capitalism, and nationalism) and a small but determined group of dissidents who have opposed these cultural themes. While this dissident thread is woven throughout America's history (via such groups as the Transcendentalists, anarchists, and progressives), it was the 1960s that first witnessed a mass cultural revolution around these themes. Discontented with the one-dimensional consumer orientation of modern industrial society, American youth (primarily, but not exclusively the children of the bourgeoisie) created a spontaneous counterculture that rejected many of the assumptions of the dominant culture. Impassioned political and social consciousness-raising generated a revitalized progressive politics that encompassed support for civil rights, a feminist movement, heightened environmental awareness, and a global peace movement. Experiments with nontraditional relationships and living arrangements altered conventional notions of marriage and the family. New perspectives in psychology (influenced by both formal research and massive informal experimentation with mind-altering chemicals) spawned a smorgasbord of mind/body therapies and self-awareness techniques, loosely grouped around the concept of a "human potential" movement. Disappointed with established and fossilized forms of religious thought, spiritual adventurers explored a spectrum of psychic experience so diverse as to include charismatic Christianity, neo-Paganism, Goddess-worship, pantheism, trance-channeling, mediumship, shamanism, and various forms of Eastern mysticism.

The dust has settled somewhat after this initial explosion of psychic-cultural energy. Some of these forms have been woven into the fabric of the dominant culture (for example, note how the interest in whole foods and vegetarianism associated with the hippie movement is now reflected in government dietary directives). Some of the cultural forms, such as the environmental movement, have become viable, oppositional political programs. Some, such as the more radical forms of feminism, genuinely alternative religious worldviews, and gay liberation, continue to be marginalized and fiercely resisted by a powerful religious-political power structure. Some, such as the movement to create sustainable, land-based intentional communities, are flourishing but largely ignored by the mainstream. Certain endeavors, such as consciousness research and holistic psychotherapy, have become sophisticated academic specialties (though the battle over what counts as legitimate knowledge is raging). Perhaps most important for this analysis, given the historical moment of late capitalism, many of these strands of activity have been co-opted or exploited in some way — the material excesses of notorious New Age spiritual charlatans being only the most blatant example.

To conservative observers, this cultural chaos is a sure sign of impending doom, the Tower of Babel preceding the demise of a culture. To more radical thinkers, it is a postmodern paradise, a relativistic smorgasbord of choice and options. To most people, it is just plain confusing. One way to understand the phenomena of the "holistic paradigm" is as an effort to incorporate this plethora of new ideas and cultural forms into a reasonably coherent worldview capable of moving us into the 21st century. Miller suggests that the discontent of the 1960s was not just an aberrant and temporary phase in American culture, but rather

> the dawning realization that the traditional themes of American culture cannot satisfy the psychological, moral and spiritual needs of a global, post-industrial age. (Miller, 1990, p. 57)

Some holistic thinkers speak optimistically of a "paradigm shift" or a "global transformation of consciousness" signaled by these cultural developments (Capra, 1982; Ferguson, 1980). Other, more critical thinkers suggest that despite the cornucopia of diverse and novel cultural expressions, fundamental power relations in this country have not changed significantly, and some writers have criticized the underlying modernist and Eurocentric assumptions inherent in "paradigmatic thinking" (Oliver & Gershman, 1989; Berman, 1989; Gelb, 1991; Kesson, 1991). Late capitalism and the modern industrial state, while showing sure signs of structural weakness, have demonstrated a remarkable capacity to absorb dissident elements. This resilience has been the subject of study by a number of critical theorists, and the questions they raise deal with the nature of knowledge itself, the problem of subtle and pervasive forms of power, and how it is that dominant cultural forms remain resistant to genuine radical change. In the next section, we will look at one particular aspect of critical theory, the critique of reason, in order to frame a discussion of how some of the key elements of the holistic "vision" might be appropriated by the dominant culture, rather than effecting the radical social transformation it proposes.

Critical Theory and the Critique of Reason

While there are a number of conceptual threads linking critical theory and holistic thought, the central connecting theme I want to focus upon here is the critique of reason as an organizing principle. At the core of opposition to the outward forms of Western culture is a revolt against the structure of rational thought itself. One has only to look around at the incredible upsurge of interest in occultism and magic of every sort, in the mythic and transpersonal dimensions of human experience, and in the multiplicity of alternative worldviews that has proliferated in our culture in recent years, to discern a virtual explosion of nonrational modes of human consciousness.

To understand this conceptual rebellion, it might be helpful to retrace the historical development of Reason. While any epochal interpretation of the development of human consciousness tends to overgeneralize, a brief encapsulation can provide a useful framework for understanding macro phenomena such as the "consciousness revolution." In Western culture, it is generally agreed that classical logic as a way of organizing reality arose in ancient Greece. Dormant throughout much of Europe during the Middle Ages, it was largely exercised by the Church patriarchy in its efforts to provide a rational basis for the revealed scriptural knowledge that formed the basis of their theology. With the advent of empirical scientific investigations in the 16th century, logic was revived in the service of secular society. The marriage of empiricism and logic spawned an ideology which came to be known as positivism, a way of constructing knowledge that, while largely discredited philosophically, has guided the development of modernist culture.

It is important to appreciate what the new rational ideology accomplished. It challenged the dogma and rigidity of medieval Scholasticism, releasing humanity from centuries of superstition and oppression by a powerful priesthood. Nature was comprehended and brought under increasing control, harnessed to meet the growing material demands of an expanding middle class. A powerful affiliation of science, the Protestant Reformation, and a rising mercantile class shattered existing religious and civic hierarchies and paved the way for democratic forms of social organization. Enlightenment thought was essential to the development of social freedoms. Yet this new way of apprehending reality and the historic social forms such apprehension assumed contain the seeds of their own reversal.

This is a rather complex argument, but essential to understanding the contemporary rejection of Reason. In their post-Holocaust book, *The Dialectic of Enlightenment*, Horkheimer and Adorno asked why humankind, rather than entering the truly human condition promised by the Enlightenment, seemed to be sinking into a new kind of barbarism. They attributed the degeneration to the rise of what they call an "instrumental reason" that has been harnessed to a mode of production based on private profit: "The unleashed market economy was both the actual form of reason and the power which destroyed reason" (Horkheimer & Adorno, 1944, p. 90). Horkheimer contrasts this "instrumental reason" or "subjective reason" with what he calls "objective reason." Some confusion can arise here because of Horkheimer's unfamiliar use of the terms *subjective* and *objective*. He defines subjective reason as the abstract functioning of the thinking mechanism, the facilities of classification, inference, and deduction — what he calls the "utilitarian" aspect of the mind. He distinguished this from objective reason, once conceived as a spiritual power living in each person, the creative force behind ideas and things — an organizing principle inherent not only in the individual but in the objective world as well. While this ideal of reason deserves further clarification, for our purposes it is only necessary to note the distinction between a reason directed to the functional accomplishment of utilitarian ends and a reason capable of determining ends which might foster the common good.

Central to the development of the thinking in the *Dialectic* is the observation that as humans have brought nature under the increasing control of instrumental reason, nature is stripped of any inherent meaning or intrinsic value. It becomes the mere tool of humans, an object of total exploitation. But the authors remind us that the domination of nature involves the domination of ourselves: "The more devices we invent for dominating nature, the more we must serve them to survive." The resultant radical disjuncture between human subjectivity and a neutral "disenchanted" nature has transformed potentially liberating reason

> into a repressive orthodoxy, the Enlightenment into totalitarianism, (which) can be understood as the result of elements integral to this form of enlightenment itself.... The reduction of reason to an instrument finally affects even its character as an instrument. (Horkheimer, 1947, pp. 93, 97, 54)

This analysis seems especially relevant today, as technical, rational solutions seem increasingly inadequate to deal with the multiple environmental and social crises wrought by the misapplication of instrumental reason.

The subjugation of nature goes on without meaningful motive, says Horkheimer. Nature is not transcended nor reconciled, but repressed. Given the contemporary revolt against reason, we should be mindful of the possibilities here:

> Typical of the present era is the manipulation of this revolt by the prevailing forces of civilization itself, the use of the revolt as a means of perpetuating the very conditions by which it is stirred up and against which it is directed.... Civilization as rationalized irrationality *integrates the revolt of nature as another means or instrument.* (Horkheimer, 1947, p. 94)

This last point is of central importance — the notion that the revolt against instrumental reason can itself be coopted and absorbed by the dominant culture, and might, in fact, serve to sustain the status quo. Horkheimer wrote his treatise in the aftermath of Naziism, and while the Nazi analogy can be extended too far, I believe that it is important to note some important similarities between the historical moment of the rise of Fascism and the contemporary mood. There is great uncertainty about the economy; values are in flux; racism and xenophobia abound; nations are in a state of disintegration; and there is a general disenchantment with the technocratic, bureaucratic State. Moreover, the machinery of mental manipulation is incredibly more sophisticated than it was at the time of Hitler. I would like to believe that people would never again succumb to the kind of mass manipulation that they fell prey to during the Third Reich, but I am continually amazed at the willingness of thinking people to surrender their fortunes, their judgment, and their souls to the most persuasive evangelist, channeler, or charismatic politician of the moment.

The rejection of Enlightenment reason contains within it the inherent exaltation of nature as a supreme principle. Hitler appealed to the unconscious in his audiences by hinting that he could forge a power in whose name repressed nature would be lifted. In this way, repressed natural drives were harnessed to the needs of Nazi rationalism:

> In modern Fascism, rationality has reached a point at which it is no longer satisfied with simply repressing nature; rationality now exploits nature by incorporating into its own system the rebellious potentialities of nature. (Horkheimer, 1947, p. 121)

To debase thought and exalt nature is a typical fallacy of an era of rationalization. Opposing the Enlightenment by regressing to earlier stages, says Horkheimer, will not alleviate the permanent crises we have created, but can lead to ever more barbaric forms of social domination. Likewise, we are cautioned against the revival of past theories of objective reason. We live in an historical period characterized by the rapid disintegration of accepted value systems and conceptual frameworks. The existential crisis provoked by such dissolution can inspire the "recycling of medieval ontologies" for modern use — leading us to cling, for example, to Absolutist philosophies in a desperate effort to stave off chaos. But the movement from objective to subjective reason, from animism to logic, from myth to magic to empiricism is a process of development which cannot be arbitrarily reversed. The solution, from the perspective of a critical theory, is the development of a reason liberated from the shackles of both superstition and instrumentalism, a reason capable of incorporating the nonrational, suppressed aspects of consciousness without sacrificing its critical capacity. This, I believe, is also the task of holistic educators.

Developing a Critical Theory of Holistic Education

In the previous section, I have looked at some of the key premises of critical theory that might help us to analyze current cultural movements, including holistic education. They include (a) the idea that the instrumental use and exploitation of nature is intimately connected to the domination of human beings; (b) that the cultivation of instrumental, utilitarian forms of reason requires the repression of nonrational forms of consciousness; (c) that suppressed forms of nonrational consciousness can erupt with great energy and intensity; and (d) that these repressed natural drives can be co-opted and harnessed to the needs of the State (in our contemporary context, that would be the corporate state). Further, we were reminded that in times of social and conceptual crisis, there is a temptation to cling to outdated, Absolutist metaphysics. Now I will use this conceptual framework to raise some questions a critical theory might ask about the phenomena of holistic education.

Holistic thought, whether it be in the realm of medicine, spirituality, or education, challenges the particular form of Western dualism that has fostered the conceptual split between mind and body, head and heart, rational and nonrational. Such categories are, within the holistic framework, arbitrary creations of minds that have been conditioned to think in either/or categories. Restoring the wholeness of perception is a primary task of holistic educators. I am in full support of this notion, but share David Purpel's concern that many holistic educators tend to focus upon one or another neglected dimension of experience (creativity, self-understanding, the significance of dreams, etc.) at the expense of developing a comprehensive theoretical perspective in which "all the important human dimensions (that includes the social, political, economic and cultural as well as the personal) are examined in relationship to one another" (Purpel, 1992, p. 18). In the remainder of this essay, I will highlight some ways in which such a limited, individualistic focus could actually contradict the explicit social and political goals and purposes of holistic educators.

Consciousness-Raising Techniques

Holistic educators have laid their political cards on the table with the document *Education 2000: A Holistic Perspective*. In it, they express support for a global, multicultural, egalitarian education that transcends narrow national, racial, class, and cultural interests. They call for a profound shift in our relationship to the natural world and support a deep ecological educational perspective. They call for a genuine democratization of the classroom that would be reflected in student choice, free inquiry, and the encouragement of independent thinking. In these and other important ways, they have laid out a genuinely alternative social vision.

Potentially more controversial than this radical social vision, however, are the wide array of what I call "spiritual technologies" available to "transform the consciousness" of students. The effort to develop increasingly more subtle forms of awareness and to tap the unconscious mind as an educative force is an important aspect of holistic education, and I believe that we need to focus some attention on the social and political implications of these powerful new "technologies." A few examples of these new "tools" for the development of consciousness are guided imagery, suggestology, subliminal programming, accelerated learning, and super-learning. I want to make it clear that I am not criticizing any of these techniques in particular — in fact, I think some of them hold great promise for the study of learning and teaching. Within the critical framework I proposed earlier, I would suggest, however, that these approaches are neutral techniques that can either work to emancipate consciousness, sustain the status quo, or open us up to ever more subtle forms of domination. Most importantly, they are not, in themselves, an adequate foundation upon which to build a comprehensive holistic educational theory.

Let us take, as one example, the interest in developing the

image-making capacity of the mind. The capacity to imag(e)ine is certainly a key to unlocking deep wellsprings of creativity in the human mind. Artists and scientists alike have testified to its efficacy in both the development of new ideas and the solving of problems. (Most people are familiar with the well-known story of how Einstein came up with special theory of relativity while visualizing himself traveling on a cosmic ray of light.) The ability to visualize can help us to conceptualize things from multiple perspectives and engage in the construction of alternative problem-solving strategies. The radical potential of this ability is real and powerful. There is vehement opposition to this and other such educational techniques from conservative religious and political groups. While some of the objections to learning strategies such as relaxation and visualization are clothed in such religious metaphors as "keeping the devil away," I suspect that the underlying fear is that traditional church, familial, and political authority will be undermined if children are encouraged to think in alternative ways.

While I am not overly concerned about the devil slipping into the relaxed minds of children, I do want to offer a slightly different critical perspective on this issue. Consciousness-raising tools such as imagery and visualization emerged from the human potential movement that, despite its counter-cultural roots in the 1960s has proven to be fertile ground for entrepreneurial capitalists. A glance through any transpersonal human development catalog reveals advertisements for consumer goods such as cassette tapes and videos that promise not only instant enlightenment, but the acquisition of mental powers that will attract wealth and influence people. Here is just a sampling from such a catalog:

> How to think, feel and behave like a winner.
> You'll learn the powerful technique of mental imaging and experience how effective it can be in attracting wealth and prosperity.
> It gives you control of the most powerful moneymaking tool you have: the power of your inner mind.
> A visualization session will impress feelings and images of wealth deeply into your subconscious (Gateways Institute, 1990).

These vulgarizations are not the stuff of a genuinely alternative social vision, but a logical New Age extension of liberalism/individualism/capitalism. I believe this example demonstrates how easily seemingly benign tools for awakening unused mental capacities can be co-opted by powerful interests for their own ends, in this case to promote the ideals of capital accumulation, competition, and individualism. This is just one example of how a popular educational technique, visualization, has been domesticated by commodification:

> what begins as a revolutionary technique for completely altering your vision of the world becomes a supernatural imprimatur of the status quo. (Basil, 1988, p. 26)

The field of holistic education has not been immune to the creative impulses of New Age entrepreneurs. Slickly packaged and sophisticated systems of learning based on the latest "brain research" promise amazing educational results. Undoubtedly, many of these ideas have enormous potential in the field of education, and I am not suggesting that we suppress them — only that holistic educators engage in serious critical dialogue about the political and social ramifications of these new technologies.

I believe that we need to engage in a careful examination of educational methods that work primarily with the subconscious mind, vigorously debating the merits of any techniques which aim to develop a receptiveness to suggestion, such as suggestology or subliminal programming. Our lives are so permeated by suggestion (in the form of advertisements and media conditioning) that it is questionable whether or not this is an emancipating approach. It reminds me too much of Huxley's "negative utopia," in which sleeping children were inculcated with slogans promoting the system — a society in which everyone "felt mellow" but had been deprived of the capacity to think critically or to question their benevolent masters. Is that really the habit of mind we wish to promote?

The Problem of Holistic Pedagogy
Without Wider Structural Change

Another way of using critical theory to analyze holistic education is to look at some of the unintended consequences of such "ameliorative reforms" as open classrooms when they are instituted in public schools (which have an historical interest in social and intellectual stratification and ideological consensus). Michael Apple, in his book, *Ideology and Curriculum*, points out how the interest in the "whole child" for example, with its inclusion of a wider range of attributes into the usual academic curricula can actually "increase the range of attributes upon which students may be stratified" (Apple, 1990, p. 142). In other words, when larger structural issues such as achievement criteria and the control of public knowledge forms go unrecognized, and when the basic goals of the institution (i.e., sifting and sorting students according to "natural" talent and ability) are not altered, potentially liberating forms of pedagogy can actually function in ways that fix students' identities even more than in the traditional classroom. In an open, humanistic setting, in the absence of larger structural change, students could conceivably be labeled on such criteria as empathy, creativity, physical grace, communication, and social skills as well as intellectual abilities. Such attributes and talents characterize children who have had the privilege of early dance, art, drama, and music experiences as well as supervised social activities — all of which require a certain income level and interested, involved adults. Such attributes, if they become part of the educational contract, should be examined for the "cultural capital" they represent, so that holistic educators do not unwittingly contribute to an even more powerful program of stratification than the one in place. This example suggests that holistic educators need to recognize the necessity for structural social and institutional changes to complement a more expansive pedagogy. In all fairness, the authors of *Education 2000: A Holistic Perspective* have called for a rethinking of grading, assessment, and standardized testing — definitely a step in the right direction.

Knowledge Forms and Social Class

In the 1980s, Jean Anyon published her research on the educational experience and curriculum knowledge that is made available to students in different social classes (1980). Her analysis of "working-class," "middle-class," "affluent professional," and "executive elite" schools reveals a disturbing relationship between the knowledge forms offered to children in schools and their probable future employment. The relevance of this study to the present paper is that it reveals the degree to which the language and purposes of the human potential/holistic education movement has already been appropriated by mid-upper echelon schools.

Anyon's study found procedures in working-class schools to be mostly mechanical, involving rote behavior and little decision making or choice. Likewise, working-class jobs are characterized by routine, mechanized, and fragmented work tasks. The middle-class schools she looked at emphasized right answers, good grades, and increased choice and decision making, with creativity peripheral to academic activities. Coincidently, lower level white collar jobs necessitate a measure of planning and decision making, but exercise no real control over the content of work. As we move up to the affluent professional school, work is "creative activity carried out independently.... Work involves individual thought and expressiveness, expansion and illustration of ideas, and choice of appropriate methods and materials." The work in the affluent professional schools corresponds nicely with the expectations of middle- and upper-class managerial and professional groups, for whom work often involves a high level of conceptualization and creativity. Moving into the rarefied atmosphere of the executive elite school, we find an emphasis on developing one's analytical powers. In a highly individualized way, children are continually asked to reason through problems, to think critically about relevant social issues and to produce intellectual products that are both logically sound and of top academic quality. Likewise, the work of the capitalist is almost entirely focused on conceptualization, planning, managing, and controlling a large enterprise.

This very brief summary of Anyon's work illuminates the extent to which many of the aims and goals of holistic educators mesh nicely with the educational agenda of the upper classes in our society. Much of the rhetoric of reform in recent years, not just that of holistic educators, has called for increased emphasis on decision making, creative problem solving, flexibility and cooperative learning. Many holistic educators seem naively optimistic when corporations and government groups embrace their ideas enthusiastically, tending to view such acceptance as evidence of a general "paradigm shift" toward greater authenticity and human values. A critical perspective might see it as the historical continuation of the complex and problematic relationship between the needs of business and the business of schools. Some questions generated from an understanding of this type of analysis could include:

> What are the political consequences of rich suburban schools adopting "super-learning" techniques if working class schools continue using rote methods?
>
> Which families are likely to choose holistic models of education if a "choice" or "voucher" system is initiated? Why?
>
> To what degree does an emphasis on harmony and unity in the classroom subsume issues of difference in the interest of developing a common culture (and whose culture will that be)? (Giroux, 1988)
>
> If higher order thinking is to be the agenda of American schools, what should

be the agenda of Korean-Philippine-Haitian education? (After all, in a post-industrial society, someone, somewhere still has to manufacture the goods.)

Critical Theory and the "Process Curriculum"

At the first annual holistic education conference, participants almost unanimously agreed that holistic educators should emphasize "process" over "content." This is undoubtedly a reaction to the externally imposed curriculum, the "banking style" of education justifiably criticized by Paulo Freire (1970). While "inquiry" (skills and methods which enable students to seek and find answers to their own questions) is undoubtedly superior to the rote methods of teaching that have prevailed in the past, Michael Apple points out how the method can actually depoliticize the study of social life, if the educator is not willing or able to engage the students in the study of *whose* knowledge they have discovered, who selected it and made it available, why it is organized the way it is, how it is maintained, and who benefits from it (Apple, 1990, p. 7). It is in this shared analysis that the educational experience might become truly transformative.

Much of the criticism of "open" or "humanistic" or "holistic" education has been directed toward its perceived lack of academic rigor. I would suggest that this is partly due to the acritical position of some advocates of the "child-centered" curriculum, who in their desire not to impose adult directives upon students, fail to work with them to uncover why particular social forms exist, how they are maintained, and who benefits from them. A truly transformative education could be a mutual and collective effort to unveil the hidden codes embedded in the everyday experience of the students which explicate the underlying paradigm that frames their present reality.[3] Beyond this decoding of the common reality structures, educators could then work with students to enable them to actively participate in the reconstruction of their social reality. This approach to education is not a content-free and nebulous "process," but a concerted critical intellectual effort to make knowledge itself "problematic" and work with students to unmask areas of taken-for-granted reality. This is a very different approach to the transformation of the social world than one which attempts to initiate students into a new "paradigm" or reality structure through subliminal or subconscious methods.

Educators occupy a sensitive role in childrens' lives. As mediators of cultural experience, they dwell in the nexus of the "subjective" worlds of children and the "objective" world of cultural experience. For too long the inner world of children has been suppressed or denied, and this is a serious flaw in our educational thinking that holistic educators seek to remedy. In our enthusiasm to nurture the subjectivities of children, I hope we don't forget that it is in the intermediate world of symbols and shared mutual dialogue that genuine cultural transformation will occur. If holistic education were nothing more than a sophisticated new bag of tricks to improve brain function, enhance narcissism, and promote an individualistic "be all you can be" mentality, then educators would do well to distance themselves from it. If it were to become a platform for promoting new orthodoxies or particular arcane systems of thought (medieval ontologies), then there is no room for it in the public education discourse. But if it realizes its own potential, which is to develop the capacity to reason critically and compassionately, incorporating and transcending dualistic and suppressed forms of consciousness to achieve a more fully developed mode of awareness, then it will serve us well as we move into the 21st century.

James MacDonald reminded us that the split between "poetics" and critical theory is one of sibling rivalry rather than a fundamental schism. He said that science, critical theory, and the mytho-poetic are *all* contributing methodologies to a larger hermeneutic circle of a continual search for greater understanding. It is in this spirit that I suggest an alliance (or at least a conversation) between the powerful interpretive analysis of critical theory and the transformative vision of holistic thought.

References

Anyon, J. (Winter, 1980). Social class and the hidden curriculum of work. *Journal of Education 162*,1, 67–92.

Apple, M. W. (1990). *Ideology and curriculum.* New York: Routledge.

Basil, R. (Ed.), (1988). *Not necessarily the new age.* New York: Prometheus Books.

Bellah, R. N. (1981). Cultural vision and the human future. In Douglas Sloan (ed.), *Toward the recovery of wholeness: Knowledge, education and human values.* New York: Teachers College Press.

Berman, M. (1989). *Coming to our senses: Body and spirit in the hidden history of the west.* New York: Simon & Schuster.

Capra, F. (1982). *The turning point.* New York: Simon & Schuster.

Clark, E. T., Jr. (Summer, 1991). Holism: Implications of the new paradigm. *Holistic Education Review 4*(2).

Ferguson, M. (1980). *The aquarian conspiracy: Personal and social transformation in the 1980's*. Los Angeles: Tarcher.

Freire, P. (1970). *Pedagogy of the oppressed*. New York: Herder & Herder

Gateways Institute, Jonathan Parker's. P.O. Box 1778, Ojai, CA 93023.

Gelb, S. (Summer, 1991). Not necessarily the new paradigm: Holism and the future. *Holistic Education Review* 4(2).

Gibson, B., & Gareth, M. (1979). *Sociological paradigms and organizational analysis: Elements of the sociology of corporate life*. Portsmouth, NH: Heinemann. Quoted by Hills in the *Journal of Curriculum Supervision*, Fall, 1991.

Giroux, H. A. (1988). *Teachers as intellectuals: Toward a critical pedagogy of learning*. Granby, MA: Bergin & Garvey.

Held, D. (1980). *Introduction to critical theory: Horkheimer to Habermas*. Berkeley: University of California Press.

Horkheimer, M. (1947). *Eclipse of reason*. New York: Oxford University Press.

Horkheimer, M., & Adorno, T. (1944). *Dialectic of enlightenment*. New York: Seabury.

Kesson, K. (Winter, 1991). The unfinished puzzle: Sustaining a dynamic holism. *Holistic Education Review* 4(4).

MacDonald, J. B. (n.d.). Theory-practice and the hermeneutic circle. In W. F. Pinar (Ed.), *Contemporary curriculum discourses*. Scottsdale, AZ: Gorsuch Scarisbrick.

Miller, R. (1990). *What are schools for? Holistic education in American culture*. Brandon, VT: Holistic Education Press.

Oliver, D., & Gershman, K. (1989). *Education, modernity and fractured meaning: Toward a process theory of teaching and learning*. Albany: SUNY Press.

Purpel, D. E. (Spring 1992). Bridges across muddy waters: A heuristic approach to consensus. *Holistic Education Review* 5(1).

Notes

1. These ideas are laid out in the report *Education 2000: A Holistic Perspective*, available from the Global Alliance for Transforming Education, 4202 Ashwoody Trail, Atlanta, GA 30319.

2. Ideas about holism are drawn from such diverse disciplines as quantum physics, ecology, Jungian psychoanalysis, transpersonal psychology, various forms of Eastern mysticism, esoteric Western spiritual traditions, eco-feminism and systems theory — a truly eclectic array of thinking. Most of the holistic literature rejects mechanism and dualism, though many holistic thinkers support dualistic epistemologies with their notion of a nonlocal mind. This contradiction, however, is beyond the scope of this paper.

3. One of the most informative and provocative analyses of this methodology of education can be found in Bowers, C.A. (1984). *The promise of theory: Education and the politics of cultural change*. New York: Teachers College Press.

Chapter 6

Toward Living Knowledge: A Waldorf Perspective

Jeffrey Kane

A number of years ago, a leading artificial intelligence expert at MIT, Dr. Joseph Weizenbaum, developed a computer program, "ELIZA," which could mimic the therapeutic technique of a Rogerian therapist. While his original intention in the development of the program was to demonstrate a method of interacting with the computer through the use of the English language, he was startled to learn that members of the psychiatric community argued that programs of this sort could be used as a primary therapeutic measure (Weizenbaum, 1976, p. 5). Incredulous, Weizenbaum asked, "What must a psychiatrist who makes such a suggestion think he is doing while treating a patient, that he can view the simplest mechanical parody of a single interviewing technique as having captured anything of the essence of human encounter" (Weizenbaum, 1976, p. 6).

The implications of Weizenbaum's question transcend issues relating to psychiatry. At its core, the question asks what the nature and meaning of human experience is relative to knowledge and thinking. Is there more to human knowledge than discreet and explicit bits of information that can be captured and stored in electronic circuitry? Is there more to thinking than the processing of information according to formal, logical patterns? Is there some aspect of human experience, of human being, that embodies a richness and depth of meaning that both animates and defies the explicit and the formal?

These questions have particular significance for educational theory in that they require us to refine our understanding of knowledge and thinking. As we answer them, we define education itself with its various objectives, priorities, and strategies.

Knowledge as Information

Howard Gardner, in his most recent book, *The Unschooled Mind: How Children Think and How Schools Should Teach* (1992), observes,

> In schools — including "good" schools — all over the world, we have come to accept certain performances as signals of knowledge or understanding. If you answer questions on a multiple-choice test in a certain way or carry out a problem set in a specified manner, you will be credited with understanding. No one ever asks the further question "But do you *really* understand?" (Gardner, 1992, p. 6)

Despite extensive research in the areas of curriculum development and educational technology, despite the efficiency of various instructional methods and the creation of new instructional tools, the concept of knowledge continues to be passive and impersonal. The assumption often embodied in such educational innovations is that knowledge consists of information that one has acquired. Knowledge in this sense is a possession rather than a generative aspect of intelligence. As a possession, it is isolated, it consists of a particular content. Yet, with its lack of integration within the intelligence itself as a focusing lens, as a means of conception and perception, as an active component in a vision of some aspect of the world, such knowledge is decontextualized and static within the emerging mind. Knowledge, as such, is information, an end to itself; it is an answer to a question. It is not, however, a means of interpretation or a basis for the initiation of new patterns of ideas or thoughts; it is not a question in search of an answer; it is not an integral, invigorating aspect of the person as he attempts to make sense of the world or some small part of it.

Recognizing this passive model of knowledge, some educational theorists have focused their efforts on the development of strategies to teach critical thinking and problem-solving skills. Often, the instructional strategies and curricular designs devoted to thinking skills take as their purpose the animation of otherwise decontextualized information. In a manner similar to computer programs that function independent of particular content, critical thinking and problem-solving programs offer generic systems for analyzing information. Unfortunately, proponents of such programs fail to account for the complex dynamics of human experience that transcend language and that are, therefore, incapable of direct representation in an explicit format. Furthermore, they overextend the role of logic in arriving at an understanding of how the world operates (a topic to be discussed at a later point in this paper). In the final analysis, the concepts of knowledge as information and thinking as logical analysis are to education what Weizenbaum's ELIZA is to psychiatry: they lack the depth, complexity, permeability, and generative insight that can derive from, and only from, human experience and human being.

If we hope that future generations will, through education, acquire meaningful knowledge and develop the capacity to think, perhaps our first task as educators is to understand what we mean by these very terms. In this context, the philosophical foundations of Waldorf education provide a unique opportunity to explore and challenge often unrecognized and unquestioned assumptions that undergird much of modern education. They offer an invaluable contrast to the assumptions of educational theory and practice.

The Waldorf Schools

Early in this century, a German industrialist, Emil Molt, the owner of the Waldorf Astoria Cigarette Factory in Stuttgart, Germany, asked Rudolf Steiner to create a school for the children of the factory's workers. Rudolf Steiner (1861–1925) was a philosopher and scientist who, in developing Wolfgang Von Goethe's worldview, was able to wed spiritual vision and scientific inquiry. Molt hoped (and was not disappointed) that Steiner could bring his insights to bear on education as he had in other fields such as medicine and agriculture. In 1919, a nonsectarian, co-educational school based upon Rudolf Steiner's philosophy was opened — the first of what has now become a worldwide community of approximately 500 Waldorf schools.

Visitors to a Waldorf school are often deeply impressed by the vivid water color paintings that line the corridors, by the richness of the music programs, by the introduction of foreign languages through song and game in the beginning grades, by the absence of textbooks, by a unique emphasis on the imaginative quality of the children's literature curriculum including fairy tales, fables, legends, and myths.

However, Waldorf education cannot be properly understood through reference to its curriculum or instructional methods, as distinctive and impressive as they may be. At the core of the school, underlying the curriculum and methods, is Rudolf Steiner's conception of the human being and human knowledge. It is in his vision of the unity of the spiritual and physical domains of existence that we find the source of the pedagogy and the impulse to continually transform technique to make education responsive to the reality of the children in the classrooms.

While Gardner explains that his concern for "genuine understanding" is not metaphysical, the contrary is true for Waldorf education: Modern education theory is problematic primarily because of its reductionistic and materialistic assumptions. In Waldorf schools "genuine understanding" is possible only when we engage, in our thinking, the active ideas that form and exist beyond the empirical world.

Knowledge as Understanding

In contrast to the metaphysical assumptions of much of modern education, Waldorf education is predicated on the notion that ideas are not limited to abstractions derived from sensory experience. More significantly, ideas exist as generative forces in nature and the human being himself. Steiner (1968, xvi) writes, "Because of man's attitude in the act of knowing, it appears as if the thoughts of things were within man, whereas in reality they hold sway within the things themselves." To attain knowledge is not to abstractly deconstruct the physical world or a particular object, but to recognize the formative ideas that give it its distinctive characteristics. To know something is to actively penetrate the ideas that weave through the object; it is to vividly incorporate them in the activity of our own thinking.

Consider the equation, "$E=mc^2$," five simple symbols representing both the foundations of the physical universe and the height of scientific sophistication. It is an equation that attests to the capacity of human intelligence, not to merely provide a calculus of empirical observations, but to approach the nonempirical ideas — the laws, the formative principles — that govern the observed and observable. These ideas transcend particular perceptions (and indeed, all perceptions collectively) and anticipate unprecedented empirical observations under circumstances beyond our current experience. The fact that relativity theory can lawfully anticipate the interaction of energy and matter, that it can grasp the idea that both bonds them and gives them their distinct nature — is the cornerstone of its claim to objectivity.

It is essential to note in this regard that the scientific community, when presented by physicist D.C. Miller with substantial evidence inconsistent with the implications of relativity, rejected the empirical data "in the hope that it would one day turn out to be wrong." (Polanyi, 1958, p. 13). The community's faith in the objectivity of the theory was found to be well placed as subsequent research revealed that Miller did not account for variables that were unknown at the time of his work. It is equally true, however, that the faith of a scientific community in a given paradigm can lead to the rejection of valuable data in the hopes that it will one day be proven false.

Although the assertion that ideas undergird and weave through nature may seem antithetical to modern thought, it was at the heart of the Copernican revolution and the very birth of science; although Ptolemaic theory provided a reasonably accurate mathematical description of the movement of planets, Copernican theory did so with greater intellectual efficiency with but one major expense — it contradicted fundamental empirical evidence. More specifically, Copernicus, believing as he did that the universe was constructed in accordance with mathematical principles, sought not merely to describe the celestial motion, but rather to reveal or "discover" the creative mathematical ideas undergirding the universe. His Pythagorean metaphysic beliefs led him to search for perfect geometrical patterns in the heavens to the point where he disregarded the clear empirical observation of the looping or epicyclical motion of the planets. E.A. Burtt states that

> it is safe to say that even had there been no religious scruples whatever against the Copernican astronomy, sensible men all over Europe, especially the most empirically minded, would have pronounced it a wild appeal to accept the premature fruits of an uncontrolled imagination.... Contemporary empiricists, had they lived in the sixteenth century, would have been first to scoff out of court the new philosophy of the universe. (Burtt, 1924, p. 38)

Copernican theory thus deferred what the eye could perceive in the physical world to what the mind could conceive in the world of formative ideas. The claim that Copernican theory had greater objective value than Ptolemaic theory was clearly not relative to empirical considerations but to the fact that it could provide a consistent and cohesive accounting of planetary motion from positions on and off the earth — something Ptolemaic theory, being circumscribed by empirical observation, could not do.

Although the meaning of the Copernican revolution and the birth of science has most often been portrayed as a battle between faith and reason, between metaphysical beliefs and empirical information, between rationality and irrationality, Copernican theory was revolutionary because it asserted that the human mind, independent of the Church, could apprehend reality. Copernican theory, by its very existence, constituted an argument that the human mind was not only capable of operating on a physical domain, but also of understanding the workings of fundamental metaphysical ideas.

While it may be argued that Copernicus based his theory on false assumptions regarding the perfect circularity of planetary motion, his ideas nonetheless provided unparalleled intellectual substance and perspective for his scientific successors. He created an intellectual focus not limited to empirical data but open to formative ideas as they pertain to the empirical world. Consequently, the eventual problem with Copernican theory was not necessarily that the concept of circularity was inappropriately applied, but rather that the interaction of ideas as they create the world was more complex than Copernicus had imagined. Just as D.C. Miller unwittingly skewed his test results by failing to account for unknown but significant variables, Copernicus was unaware of other formative ideas such as those that may be expressed under the concept of gravity that could stretch a circle into an ellipse.

These arguments regarding Copernican and relativity theory should not be interpreted as a disputation of the value of empirical information or mathematical analysis. Rather, they are intended to illustrate that science, at its birth and at its 20th century heights, is not circumscribed by, and ultimately does not refer to, empirical facts but ideas. These ideas, as they are symbolically represented through mathematics, are abstractions; as they exist in the world they are vital, creative forces. It is the object of science to envision and represent the flow of these ideas, their fluid movement in the empirical world, rather than generate static pictures of particular empirical fields. Just as the Copernican elucidation of the motion of the planets was derived primarily from his Pythagorean beliefs, so relativity theory derived from Einstein's imaginative conceptions of the nature of the universe as perceived by a traveller moving at the speed of light. The creative flow of the imaginations of these scientists was the source of their insight, and their *genius lay in their capacity to merge their creative grasp of formative ideas with empirical observation.*

The abstract mathematical characteristic of their work constitutes a formal representation of their thinking and not the logical progression of thought itself. Michael Polanyi explains:

> Mathematical reasoning about experience must include, besides the antecedent non-mathematical finding and shaping of the experience, the equally non-mathematical relating of mathematics to such experience, and the eventual, also non-mathematical, understanding of experience elucidated by mathematical theory. Mathematical abstractions must include an active knower, carrying out and committing himself, to these non-mathematical acts of knowing. (Grene, 1969, p. 179)

Polanyi explains further, "Mathematics only inserts a formalized link in a procedure which starts with an intuitive surmise of a significant shape, and ends with an equally informal decision to reject or accept it as truly significant" (Grene, 1969, p. 108).

Post-Einsteinian physics has now progressed where the fluid ideas that weave through empirical fields can no longer be expressed in terms of explicit, mathematical statements. Contemporary physicist David Bohm states:

> The new form of insight can perhaps best be called *undivided wholeness in flowing movement.* This view implies that flow is, in some sense, prior to that of the "things" that can be seen to form and dissolve in this flow.... [T]here is a universal flux that cannot be defined explicitly but which can be known only implicitly, as indicated by the explicitly definable forms and shapes, some stable and some unstable, that can be abstracted from the universal flux. In this flow, mind and matter are not separate substances. Rather, they are different aspects of one whole and unbroken movement. (Bohm, 1980, p. 11)

Such a model of knowledge does not end with explicit mathematical formulae describing the interaction of discreet bits of matter but with personal implicit understanding of an "implicate order." *Knowledge, at this level, consists of the mind dwelling in formative idea itself.*

At this point, we should note that our discussion has thus far focused on knowledge in physics because it is for our present purposes, the easiest scientific discipline to understand. While we often think of physics in terms of the most sophisticated theoretical foundations of all the sciences, it is nonetheless the case that the formative ideas governing physical reality are less complex than those, let us say, in the area of biology. When we enter a discipline such as biology, we encounter an enormous number of formative ideas over and above those active in physics. As we move from mineral to plant to animal to human being, we add formative laws that overlay and interact with one another. When considering plants, we must address the fact they are living entities; when considering animals, we must address the fact that they have sophisticated physical and emotional sensory capacities; when considering human beings, we must address the fact that we also have a capacity for reflection and conscious identity. The capacity to understand the formative ideas working at each successive level requires evermore vivid, yet precise, imagination. Gregory Bateson, attempting to provide a unified, cohesive vision of these factors, can go no further than to speak of "the pattern which connects." In his quest, he observes,

> I hold to the presupposition that our loss of the sense of aesthetic unity was, quite simply, an epistemological mistake. I believe that mistake may be more serious than all the minor insanities that characterize those older epistemologies which agreed upon the fundamental unity. (Bateson, 1979, p. 19)

We can perhaps best understand such a concept by way of an analogy to music. As we listen to a piece of music, we recognize that every note and chord is shaped by and carries a meaning that transcends it. An analysis of the frequency, amplitude, and duration of an individual note would tell us little about the factors that brought it to its particular state; a calculus of the physical characteristics of the chords would not reveal the idea that wove them. Our understanding of the music, other than with reference to its comparative structure and content, derives from our ability to imaginatively dwell *in* the meaning within and beyond the sound waves that reach our ears.

Just as a piece of music is best understood by imaginatively experiencing the meaning which runs in and through it, so empirical phenomena are best understood by dwelling *in* the creative ideas that form them. This is not to suggest that all human knowledge is derived in this fashion, for indeed, we spend the majority of our lives abstracting, classifying, and sorting empirical information. The intellectual structures we create enable us to organize and order the world around us; they enable us to develop a rational context within which to operate and cope. This approach to understanding the natural world maximizes the efficiency of our action; we learn to identify the problems we face whether in terms of our need for electrical power, rapid communication, or medical innovation and develop solutions which will effectively serve our interests. In this context, the principles of physics and biology are circumscribed by practical dilemmas — not ideas as they exist objectively, but as they pertain to our objectives.

The problem here is that this approach to understanding distorts and limits the range of considerations we address. Rather than recognizing a unity, an implicate order, or "the pattern which connects," we segment the world into manageable units — units in which the pieces have meaning relative primarily, if not exclusively, to our intentions. This fragmentation is particularly dangerous not only because it provides a skewed and limited picture of the world; it can also rob us of our capacity to imagine the workings of ideas at higher and deeper levels of reality. Dependency on this model of knowledge is fractionalizing our conception, not only of the world, but of ourselves, both personally and socially. Bohm writes,

> our fragmentary form of thought is leading to a widespread range of crises, social, political, economic, ecological, psychological, etc. in the individual and in society as a whole. Such a mode of thought implies unending development of chaotic and meaningless conflict, in which the energies of all tend to be lost by the movements that are antagonistic or else at cross-purposes. (Bohm, 1980, p. 16)

As Ralph Waldo Emerson said over a century ago, "The reason why the world lacks unity, and lies broken and in heaps, is, because man is disunited with himself" (Spiller, 1971, p. 43).

Education as Transformation

Waldorf education begins with the understanding that knowledge of the sort described above — living knowledge — is both informative and educative. It is informative in the sense that it gives form to the flow of thought; it is educative in the sense that it draws forth and engages the mind in the act of knowing. In this context, knowledge is an active force, a generative power, not in nature only, but in the human being himself. As a student acquires knowledge, the imagination is spurred. The child stretches to understand; he seeks, through his own activity, to experience as a means a comprehension, the creative forces that shape the world. Thus, he is not only informed, but actively transformed — the ideas he has engaged actively shape his body, character, and mind.

Rudolf Steiner observes,

> Our civilization is calculated to make men cognize everything with their heads. Ideas rest in the head as upon a couch. The ideas are at rest in the head as though they lay in bed. They are asleep; they only "mean" this or that. We carry them stored up in us as in so many little pigeon-holes and otherwise we

want to have nothing to do with them. At the Waldorf School, the children do not merely "have an idea" in their heads; they feel the idea, for it flows into their whole life of feeling. Their being of soul lives in the sense of the idea, which is not merely a concept but becomes a plastic form. The whole complex of ideas at last becomes human form and figure and in the last resort all this passes over into the will. The child learns to transform what he thinks into actual deed. (Steiner, 1972, p. 198)

Experience of an idea at this level is beyond language. The capacity to analyze or critically assess an idea should, ideally, derive from and articulate such experience at a time appropriate to a child's development. However, explication and analysis can, in no way, substitute for the activity of the idea as a vital aspect of intelligence itself. Experience of this sort is based upon encounter, rather than control, respect rather than manipulation, understanding rather than utility.

At its core, the concept of knowledge that undergirds Waldorf education consists of the imaginative play with the generative forces that continuously recreate the world. As one experiences, one dwells dynamically in these forces, coming to know them through creative effluence rather than detached analyses.

The imagination, here, is not fanciful — a pouring forth of subjective impressions. It is a bridging of conception and perception — a recognition of the fluid energies, ideas, that course through inanimate objects, plans, animals, and human beings (individually and collectively). The imagination is the creative attempt, in active thought prior to language, to dwell in the movement of the creative forces at work in the world. Through the imagination, we perceive a plant, for example,

not merely externally, but to participate in all its processes, so that our thinking joins in the life of the external world. We are to sink into the plant to feel how gravity goes down the root into the earth, how formative forces unfold above ground; we are to feel from the inside the blooming and fruiting. (Richards, 1980, p. 79)

Explicit thoughts and rational intellectual structures may and often do rise from imaginative perception. The fluid can be made static; dynamic interactions can be classified; personal insight can be fixed in terms appropriate for public discussion and logical analysis. However, the process of articulation in such cases is partial and lacking in generative quality; they have been created by living thought, but are themselves lifeless. Such explicit formal concepts are of little value if they fail to invigorate and enhance the individual's ability to develop imaginative insight into the vital forces that weave through the perceptible. As such, they have but limited educative value.

Given this perspective, Waldorf education does *not* focus on the transmission of information or on the critical analysis of particular problems. Intellectual processes of this sort can prematurely fix ideas in the child's mind and reduce his capacity to dwell within them. The child who has been taught to articulate thoughts and employ logical processes in the development of rational structures will not likely have the living insight which transcends and gives abstract ideas their meaning. In Steiner's words,

> Nothing more harmful can be done to a child than to awaken too early his independent judgment. Man is not in a position to judge until he has collected in his inner life material for judgment and comparison. If he forms his conclusions before doing so, his conclusions will lack foundation.

> The thought must take living hold in the child's mind, that he has first to learn and then to judge.... Before that time, the intellect has only an intermediary part to play: its business is to grasp what takes place and is experienced in feeling, to receive it exactly as it is, not letting the unripe judgment come in at once and take possession. (Steiner, 1965, p. 46)

The Waldorf school curriculum, consequently, is not constructed to acquaint children with particular factual material or critical thought processes. Rather, all subjects provide an occasion for imaginative perception and conception, as well as the foundation of a personal, active foundation for understanding. Each subject is selected to educe the imagination and provide a developmentally appropriate form for such activity.

Let us consider three examples of Waldorf pedagogy: (a) the introduction to the letters, (b) the introduction to multiplication tables, and (c) the teaching of Renaissance history.

Introduction to the Letters

In the Waldorf school, children are introduced to the letters through fairy tales and artistic activity. Fairy tales provide metaphors for the creative ideas that give scope and meaning to humanity. Through the fairy tale, the child is provided an imaginative foundation for weaving a coherent sense of who he is and what the world is like. Franz Winkler explains,

> When we tell a fairy tale to a child, we must never forget that it deals primarily with man's inner life, his soul life. Its characters represent psychological qualities rather than people of flesh and blood. Its kingdoms are not of this world; they symbolize the vast, partly hidden realms of the human soul. In

these realms, unselfish will and purified emotion must find their union as prince as princess, to rule their domain with the help of reason grown into wisdom. (Winkler, 1960, p. 206)

With the fairy tales as the living meaning undergirding language, the children address the creation of the letters. Following each story, the teacher and children draw a simple, colorful illustration. This illustration for the story of "The Seven Swans," for example, might be of swans on a lake. With the teacher's drawing before the class, the teacher gradually transforms the figure of the swan into the letter 'S'.

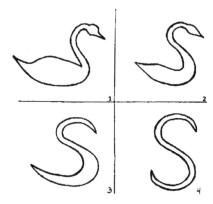

The *symbol* of the letter is *symbolic* precisely because it represents in abstract form a picture, an image beyond itself as well as a sound. In moving from the picture to the letter form, the child shifts from the domain of the creative idea to the created object.

In addition, children begin to recognize that written language arises in a creative human context. While it may be argued that the letter 'S' did not originate with the story of the swans, it is nonetheless true that our Roman alphabet arose through a gradual cultural transformation of pictures, cuneiform, into the abstract symbols we recognize today. The 26 letters that compose our alphabet are not so many combinations of straight and curved lines, but are the embodiment of the human effort to transform ideas into public symbols. Although all such considerations lie far beyond recognition by the children (who quite simply take joy in the lessons), their experience of written language is vivid and meaningful, while their appreciation of the written symbol is enhanced.

Introduction to the Multiplication Tables

One of the most essential aspects of Waldorf pedagogy with respect to the teaching of arithmetic is that children develop a recognition of the order and complex symmetries of number. Consequently, arithmetic is not approached pragmatically, but rather with a respect for the patterns and relationships of numbers. Often, the multiplication tables are introduced by walking rhythmically and counting out the tables. For example, an introduction to the two-times table might consist of the stomping of one's foot on every second step and a corresponding shout at every even number. The children are encouraged to experience, often through movements, the relationship between the rhythms of the tables and the commonality of abundant numbers. In this way, children quite literally learn the multiplication tables by heart — by moving rhythmically like the beating heart — and acquire a direct and creative understanding of the dynamics patterns that weave through number.

Building upon such lessons, children may be encouraged to find more complex and varied patterns in the multiplication tables. For example, they might aesthetically dwell on the symmetries of various multiplication tables in the ones digit place and represent the patterns in number circles. (See Figure 2 below)

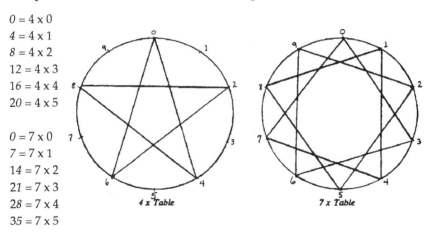

$0 = 4 \times 0$
$4 = 4 \times 1$
$8 = 4 \times 2$
$12 = 4 \times 3$
$16 = 4 \times 4$
$20 = 4 \times 5$

$0 = 7 \times 0$
$7 = 7 \times 1$
$14 = 7 \times 2$
$21 = 7 \times 3$
$28 = 7 \times 4$
$35 = 7 \times 5$

Figure 2. The drawings above are representations of the patterns formed by the ones digits (in the products) in the four and seven multiplication tables. A line is drawn from each successive number in the ones digit patterns to the next number in the sequence. For example, in the 4 times table successive lines are drawn from the 0 to the 4, from the 4 to the 8, from the 8 to the 2, from the 2 to the 6 and from the 6 to the 0 to complete the pattern. The circles within which the lines are drawn are circular 0 - 9 number lines.

Lest we minimize the value of such insight, let us recall the story told of the young Gauss who was asked by his teacher to add the numbers between 0 and 100. Gauss almost immediately responded with the correct answer, 5,050, and explained that he had arrived at the sum by recognizing the symmetries of the numbers between 0 and 100. More specifically, he reasoned that he could create fifty pairs of numbers such as 0 and 100, 99 and 1, 98 and 2, etc., all equalling 100, with the number 50 remaining uncoupled. With the fifty pairs of 100 equaling 5000, the 50 remaining was added. The discovery of young Gauss was possible because his imagination enabled him to perceive patterns and relationships that others, perhaps more pragmatic than he, might never have noticed.

The Teaching of the Renaissance

The history of curriculum in the Waldorf schools is designed to introduce children to historical periods that reflect in their consciousness, their Zeitgeist, the developmental stages of the children themselves. The particular facts, the names and dates in the chronology of human events, are less significant than the fact that different historical periods embody varied modes of thinking, conceptions of individuality, and systems of social interaction. The study of history is, in essence, an exploration of a macrocosmic drama in which children can get a larger picture of themselves within and of the world around them.

The Renaissance was an age in which the "individual" began to explore with far greater freedom than had been known before the potentials of his own mind. Science, a mode of inquiry that challenged the established intellectual authority of the Church, flourished. New, more individuated religious conceptions began to emerge. The arts blossomed in the hands of magnificently gifted artists.

It is with this sense of renewed self, of self-discovery, of the emergence of a new level of individuality, that the Renaissance is introduced to seventh graders who themselves are breaking away from the established authority of their parents, as well as discovering new and varied aspects of themselves and beyond. Recognizing the emergence of the multidimensional individual, the teaching of the Renaissance in Waldorf schools focuses on the biographies of the leading individuals. The stories of the great painters are told, and often children draw intricate copies of the work of a master painter.

In this way, the children begin to see the world through the master's eyes. They see parallels between their own lives and the conflict and promise of the lives of the great painters. In the act of drawing with more focus and specificity than they had before imagined, the children begin to inwardly move through the passions and creative spirit at the heart of the Renaissance. The meaning of the Renaissance to children who have been taught in this fashion is not to be found only in the historical information which sheds light on our tradition and culture, but also in the exploration of the interior landscapes of our own humanity — landscapes that might have remained unexplored had the children not been guided through them by genius of the masters.

Imagination and the Person

Waldorf educational theory begins with the understanding that thinking is rooted in being and that learning should compliment imaginative and intellectual activity with an experience of appreciation, of wonder, of loving encounter.

As one imaginatively encounters the world, one experiences reverence, gratitude, and awe for the genius of the natural world. The concept of feeling here should not be confused with that of sentiment. Feeling, in this context, does not begin with the subjective tastes or inclinations of the individual, but rises from within as a recognition of the vital forces, infinitely varied and complex, at work in the world. If we can listen in awe to the grace of Bach or power of Beethoven, how much more have we cause to appreciate the order and wonder of the world. As Emerson writes, "the invariable mark of wisdom is to see the miraculous in the common. To the wise, therefore, a fact is true poetry, and the most beautiful of fables" (Spiller, 1971, p. 44).

John Gardner explains,

> Waldorf teachers believe that a nuance of feeling and an inward gesture belonged to each perceived fact quite as objectively as does a certain concept. Just as the fact awakens thoughts in an observer and these thoughts reveal something about this fact; so, if we do not arbitrarily prevent it from doing so, this same fact will awaken, with equal necessity, configurations of feeling, and it will stir the observer in his will. Such inward experiences also reveal something about the fact. They are signs that one is dealing with the whole fact, not just with its appearance. (Gardner, 1962, p. 9)

Just as Plato maintained that flame coming forth from the eye permits perception, so a sense of awe and respect is necessary to illuminate the creative in the creative. We come to understand through warmth rather than impersonal detachment. Sheldon Stoff writes, "True feeling is not compulsive.... It does not obliterate reason but enriches it, giving it power of comprehension. There can be no dialogue without warmth; man or nature can be rightly known only through warm encounter" (Stoff, 1973, p. 25).

Undoubtedly, this is a concept which eludes modern thinking. We have so separated knowledge from a human knower that we find it difficult, if not impossible, to understand how the human qualities affect cognitive processes. While an elaboration of this point is beyond the scope of this paper, suffice it to say for present purposes that the attitude with which one approaches the world can either unveil miraculous patterns and relationships or confine perception to only those things that seem useful. Steiner, writes, "Veneration, homage, devotion are like nutriment making [the soul] healthy and strong, especially strong for the activity of cognition. Disrespect, antipathy, underestimation of what deserves recognition, all exert a paralyzing and withering effect on this faculty of cognition" (Steiner, 1947, p. 13).

The heart of the matter is that awe rather than detachment is a prerequisite for knowledge. Awe is not a reaction but a posture, a mode of address, an openness that allows encounter. Rabbi Abraham Heschel explains,

> There seem to be two courses of human thinking: one begins with man and his needs and ends in assuming that the universe is a meaningless display or a waste of energy: the other begins in amazement, in awe and humility and ends in the assumption that the universe is full of a glory that surpasses man and his mind. (Heschel, 1955, p. 105)

For those who would be concerned about the dangers of sentimentalism associated with an education devoted to the nurturing of reverence, gratitude, and awe, C.S. Lewis responds, "For every one pupil who needs to be guarded from a weak excess of sensibility, there are three who need to be awakened from the slumber of cold vulgarity. The task of the modern educator is not to cut down jungles, but to irrigate deserts" (Lewis, 1947, p. 24).

Conclusion

Waldorf pedagogy challenges the metaphysical assumptions of modern educational thought. It emphasizes a model of knowledge that is intrinsically educative. Such knowledge lies beyond words and renders them meaningful; it derives its authority from engagement with the creative ideas that weave together to create the perceptible world.

To know is not only to be informed but transformed, to be moved imaginatively, to dwell on ideas, and to let them lend their form to both our thinking and being. To learn is not merely to acquire explicit facts and figures, but to experience inwardly that which undergirds them. The object, in the final analysis, is not only to educate so that we acquire the knowledge and skills necessary to control the environment or grapple with practical problems, however large, but more fundamentally to so encounter the creative in the world that we, ourselves, come more fully into being.

References

Bateson, G. (1979). *Mind and nature.* New York: Bantam.

Bohm, D. (1980). *Wholeness and the implicate order.* London: Routledge & Kegan Paul.

Burtt, E. A. (1924). *The metaphysical foundations of modern science.* New York: Doubleday.

Gardner, H. (1991). *The unschooled mind.* New York: Basic Books.

Gardner, J. F. (1962). *The experience of knowledge.* New York: Myrin Institute.

Grene, M. (Ed.). (1969). *Knowing and being.* Chicago: University of Chicago Press.

Herschel, A. J. (1955). *God in search of man: A philosophy of Judaism.* New York: Harper & Row.

Kane, J. (1984). *Beyond empiricism: Michael Polanyi reconsidered.* New York: Lang.

Lewis, C. S. (1947). *The abolition of man.* New York: Macmillan.

McDermott, R. A. (1984). *The essential Steiner.* San Francisco: Harper & Row.

Nyberg, D. (Ed.). (1985). *Philosophy of education: 1985.* Normal, IL: Philosophy of Education Society.

Polanyi, M. (1958). *Personal knowledge.* New York: Harper & Row.

Richards, M. C. (1980). *Toward wholeness: Rudolf Steiner education in America.* Middletown, CT: Wesleyan University Press.

Sloan, D. (Ed.). (1984). *Toward the recovery of wholeness: Knowledge, education, and human values.* New York: Teachers College Press.

Spiller R. E. (1971). *The collected works of Ralph Waldo Emerson.* Vol II. Cambridge, MA: Harvard University Press.

Steiner, R. (1943). *Education and modern spiritual life.* London: Anthroposophic Press.

Steiner, R. (1947). *Knowledge of the higher worlds and its attainment.* New York: Anthroposophic Press.

Steiner, R. (1965). *The education of the child.* London: Rudolf Steiner Press.

Steiner, R. (1968). *A theory of knowledge based on Goethe's world conception.* New York: Anthroposophic Press.

Steiner, R. (1972). *A modern art of education*. London: Rudolf Steiner Press.

Stoff, S. H., & Schwartzberg H., (Eds.). (1973). *The human encounter: Readings in education*. New York: Harper & Row.

Weizenbaum, J. (1976). *Computer power and human reason*. San Francisco: Freeman.

Whitehead, A. N. (1957). *The aims of education*. New York: Free Press.

Winkler, F. E. (1960). *Man: The bridge between two worlds*. New York: Gilbert Church.

Chapter 7

The Whole of
Whole Language

Lois Bridges Bird

Whole Language as a dynamic, evolving grassroots movement among American educators is not much more than a decade old, but as a learner-centered educational philosophy that stems from such progressive pioneers as Comenius, Pestalozzi, Dewey, Kilpatrick, Lucy Sprague Mitchell, Caroline Pratt, and George S. Counts (Edelsky, Altwerger, & Flores, 1991; Goodman, Y., 1991; Miller, 1991), it spans both continents and centuries. Unlike their progressive antecedents, however, Whole Language educators draw support from an extensive scientific research base (Goodman & Goodman, 1991; Stephens, 1992) that includes a variety of disciplines and perspectives: developmental psychology, psycholinguistics, sociolinguistics, anthropology, and sociology; in fact, Whole Language establishes scientific credibility for the good intuitions progressive educators have always had about how human beings learn, how language develops and how these processes are best supported in the classroom. Whole Language is not just a new scientific way to teach reading and language arts, however; it is a philosophy that addresses the whole nature of the teaching/learning relationship within the classroom and beyond. It is a theory not only of language, learning, and teaching, but also of curriculum and community embedded within a socio-political context. Simply defined, it is a way of living and learning with students in classrooms while helping them learn to live and make a positive difference within the communities that extend beyond the classroom — the school, the neighborhood, and the global community.

For exponents of this positive, humanistic way of learning and teaching, the *whole* of Whole Language has two key meanings. The first meaning defines it as "undivided"; the second meaning defines it as "unified and integrated." This essay will explore both meanings as it examines the scientific theory underlying Whole Language, together with the role of learners, teachers, curriculum, school communities, and politics from a philosophical and applied perspective. Since Whole Language is a "theory *in* practice" (Edelsky, Alwerger, & Flores, 1991), it is often best understood within the context of real classroom experiences.

A Theory of Language

The first meaning stems from the sociopsycholinguistic theory that holds that language, whether oral or written, is most readily learned when it is kept whole and in context. *Sociopsycholinguistic* refers to the cognitive and linguistic processes underlying language and to the social context in which language always occurs. Language is a complex system for creating meaning through socially shared conventions (Halliday, 1978). Thus, "language can only mean what its community of users know — the meanings users have attached to the experiences they have had" (Edelsky, Altwerger, & Flores, 1991). In this regard, language is constantly evolving as it stretches and expands to accommodate and represent a community's new experiences (for example, all the developing terminology associated with virtual reality).

Authentic language in use always consists of four linguistic subsystems: (a) the phonological (in oral language); the graphic and graphophonic (in written); (b) the syntactic; (c) the semantic; and (d) the pragmatic. All subsystems are interdependent, working together simultaneously to support the language user. As a result, language is wonderfully predictable and redundant, offering multiple cues to narrow down the possiblities, enabling the language user to "predict anything from the next word to the gist of a whole text" (Edelsky, Altwerger, & Flores, 1991). This predictable aspect of language, so helpful to the language user, is lost when one or more of the linguistic cueing systems is stripped away, as is the case with reductionist reading materials such as phonics drills, flashcards, and basal workbooks.

This reductionist approach to literacy instruction stems from behavioral psychology's theory of learning, based on the seductive idea that to learn how to put something together you first have to take it apart. But a growing body of research across disciplines shows that children learn language, oral and written, by moving from wholes to parts; they focus on meaning before mastering the fine points of form (Ferreiro & Teberosky, 1982; Goodman, Altwerger, & Marek, 1981; Graves & Stuart, 1985; Harste, Woodward, & Burke, 1984; Teale & Sulzby, 1986). The complex, integrated processes involved in human language and learning suffer greatly when reduced to a piecemeal presentation. Language that is broken down into isolated sounds, letters, syllables, and words loses its communicative function and no longer operates like real language. It becomes little more than bite-size abstractions. The smaller the unit of language, the more abstract it becomes.

Education's alignment with behavioral psychology (Smith, 1986; Newman, 1985; Weaver, 1990) has led to programmed instruction and a component model of learning in which everything, including language, is broken down into parts. These parts comprise the skills that children are drilled on endlessly, in keeping with the behaviorists' formula for learning — stimulus, response, reinforcement. Thus, reading becomes little more than breaking down words into discrete units: initial and final consonants, vowels, blends, and the like. Reading in real books is often postponed indefinitely, until children have mastered the manipulation of these abstract bits of language, leading to what Holdaway terms, "criminal print starvation" (1979).

Writing is equally fragmented. Children begin with handwriting, practicing first the formation of individual letters before graduating to words. All succeeding drills continue in a similiar piecemeal fashion: Children memorize lists of isolated spelling words, punctuate rows of sentences copied from textbooks, diagram pages of paragraphs in their grammar books.

Whole Language educators reject the artificial splintering of language. In the teaching of reading, for example, they draw on the pioneering work of psycholinguist Ken Goodman (1965), who has revolutionized what is known about reading as an interaction between the reader and author of a text. Listening to real readers reading whole texts, Goodman conducted a linguistic analysis of their "miscues," defined as any deviation from the written text, and demonstrated that contrary to popular assumptions about reading as a precise process of word identification, it is, in fact, an active, tentative, problem-solving process in which readers use the four linguistic cueing systems in conjunction with cognitive strategies as they work to construct meaning. Readers bring their own conceptual experiences and languages to bear on the text as they engage in a mental dialogue with the author. The meaning does not reside in the text; meaning is created as the reader and author interact through the text.

As Whole Language teachers support and encourage their students to write, they rely on the research of Atwell (1987), Calkins (1986, 1991), and Graves (1983) who have clearly shown that the only way to learn how to write is to write daily, about self-selected topics that you know and care about, with numerous opportunities to share your writing with others, receive their feedback, and if appropriate, revise accordingly. Like reading, writing is a process of constructing meaning through multiple drafts. Knowledge of the conventions that support writing — correct spelling, syntax, punctuation, and the like — develop within the context of real writing. Two generations of crippled writers proves that isolated drill on these aspects of written language does not achieve the instructional objective of people who can write. Supported by their knowledge of the research, Whole Language teachers work hard to keep all language experiences whole, in context, and thus, meaningful, functional, and easy to learn.

The work of sociolinguist Michael Halliday (1975, 1978) has figured prominently in the theory underlying Whole Language. Through his functional theory of language learning, Halliday has demonstrated that students learn about language as they use language to learn. Students use reading, writing, speaking, and listening to learn about their world, to pursue questions that are of real interest to them, and in the process they learn what language is and how language works. Thus, Whole Language is integrated and unified (the second meaning of Whole Language) in the sense that children use all four language systems simultaneously as they go about the business of learning. Students explore, extend, and refine their evolving understandings as they participate in discussions, read a wide variety of material across genre and functions, and write in reflective learning logs.

A Theory of Learning

Whole Language is unified and integrated in still another way: the best traditions of progressive education — that is, education that begins with students' strengths, experiences, and interests, that enables students to learn by doing, that is as rich, meaningful, and functional as real life — are now supported by research in child language development, cognitive psychology, sociolinguistics, linguistics and anthropology. American education, dominated by behavioral psychology and scientific management theories, has a tradition of opposing scientific views to humanistic ones. The marriage of behavioral psychology and industrial management led to an obsession with controlling teachers and children through a learning technology built on textbooks, basal readers, and standardized tests (Shannon, 1989, 1990). As Goodman and Goodman contend, humanistic educators have found this union "too narrow, rigid, and dehumanizing." But they have been ridiculed as "loving rather than teaching children ... of being unscientific and opposed to progress" (Goodman, 1989).

Whole Language weds humanism and science, but unlike the laboratory-controlled science of the behavioral psychologist, the science underlying Whole Language theory is conducted in real classrooms with real students. Whole Language researchers have aligned themselves with anthropologists who advocate a naturalistic understanding of meaning. Instead of developing educational programs based on what rats do in mazes and pigeons do with pecking bars, Whole Language researchers observe children in their natural learning environments as they go about their daily business of exploring and learning about their world.

For their research methodology, many anthropologists rely primarily on ethnography, defined as the description of culture. Ethnographic research, or naturalistic inquiry, attempts to explain what is happening in a naturally occuring environment. Over the last twenty years, educational researchers have increasingly viewed ethnography as one of the most appropriate ways to study children and the ways in which they learn language and literacy. Researchers have been turning their attention from the behaviorist's experimental laboratory to the culture of the natural learning environment. They have been looking at the collaboration of parents and children and their interaction around meaningful and functional "literacy events" such as storytelling, reading story books, making shopping lists, writing letters to relatives, and sorting mail. They have been joined in their investigation by researchers from a variety of academic disciplines, including psychology.

Piaget and Vygotsky are two psychologists who have had a major impact on Whole Language understanding. Through his careful, detailed observations of children, including his own, Piaget (1952) discovered that children create their conceptual worlds through their activity with and on external objects. And the worlds that children construct are different both qualitatively and quantatively from those of the adult. The developing logic of the child is unique and different from, but not inferior to, the logic of the adult.

Whole Language teacher, Marty Morgenbesser (1991), was reminded of the importance of respecting children as capable, creative learners and trusting their logic, as he was teaching his class of seven- and eight-year-olds how to construct base ten numbers with wooden blocks. He sat next to Anna and asked her to create the number ninety-six. Normally, this would be accomplished by placing nine ten blocks to the left of six one blocks.

Instead, Anna reached for the hundred block. "Are you sure you want *that* block?" asked Marty. Anna was sure. "I want to do it a different way," she explained. Resisting the temptation to show her the "right" way, Marty watched as she placed one ten block to the left of the hundred block and added six ones to the right.

"See!" she exclaimed, "It's like a Roman numeral!" Marty was delighted. Earlier that morning, when they were discussing Roman numerals, Anna had appeared to be confused. Now she had demonstrated that she not only understood the concept, but was able to apply her knowledge in a creative, novel way. "And," continued Anna, "I can make the number ninety-six in the normal way, too!" Accordingly, she quickly rearranged the blocks into that pattern. Marty compares teaching to "improvisational theater" (1991) and remarks that "real teaching begins" when we trust children and allow them to take the lead, showing us what they know.

Whole Language educators have drawn their understanding of the social nature of learning from the work of Lev Vygotsky (1978) who highlighted the importance of play and interaction with others in relation to human conceptual and linguistic development. Vygotsky maintained that what the child can do alone is not as significant in the learning process as what he or she can do with the help of another. This is the "zone of proximal development," the new realm of knowing into which a child, with the help of another, can enter. Gloria Norton, a former elementary school resource teacher, illustrates this critical learning/teaching interaction through her work with Paul, a second grader who needed some encouragement (Bird, 1991).

When Gloria first met with Paul on November 20 his writing consisted of nonsensical letters strings.

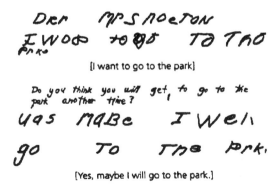

Nonetheless, Gloria engaged Paul in a written conversation and responded to each of his entries on the basis of what he explained it said. This continued for several weeks, until Gloria, having watched Paul at work on several occasions, knew that he could do more. On December 7 she said, "Paul, I want you to write so that I can read it."

The results were dramatic and instantaneous. Paul became a writer, able to use written langauge to communicate with others.

[I want to go to the park]

[Yes, maybe I will go to the park.]

In 17 days, Paul changed from a child with no confidence in his ability to write to into a child who knew he could write — and did. Gloria Norton's informed and sensitive mediation made the difference. Paul's next entry read:

We haf to

keh the kds

Be faw

thee Got
uad the taBOL

[We have to catch the kids before they get under the table.]

Why do they want to go under the table?

Saw Tha wot git tag

[So they won't get tagged.]

This vignette also illustrates once again the union of the humanistic traditions of learner-centered education — beginning with the child's strengths, building on what the child knows — with scientific research. The work of Clay (1976), Doake (1981), Ferreiro and Teberosky (1982), Y. Goodman (1984), Harste, Burke, and Woodward (1984), Teale & Sulzby (1986) reveals that the same powerful learning strategies that serve children so well in oral language learning serve them equally well in written language learning, provided that the conditions that support learning to talk are also present for learning to read and write. As Holdaway writes, "Unquestionably the most efficient learning environments we know are those centered on the conditions of the healthy home" (1984, p. 9). Parents are perfect language-learning partners. They trust that their children will eventually learn to talk. This act of faith enables them to focus on the meaning of what the child is attempting to communicate, rather than worrying about the correctness of the communicative form. Thus, parents engage in constant verbal interaction with their child, responding to, celebrating, elaborating, and extending all linguistic exploration and risk taking. Whole Language educators like Gloria Norton understand that trust in the learner, focus on meaning, and constant, sensitive interaction support children on their learning odysseys into literacy in the same way they serve to support their oral language learning.

A Theory of Curriculum

In Whole Language, not only are science and humanism unified; so also is the curriculum. Reading and language arts, math, science, and social studies — all occur simultaneously as children in Whole Language classrooms use them to learn about their world. Much like Kilpatrick's Project Method (1918), the disciplines are not broken down into isolated skills and taught in separate segments of time, but rather are used to help students conduct real-life inquiry, to pursue questions that are of real interest to them. As Dewey (1943) argued, "We do not have a series of stratified earths, one of which is mathematical, another physical, another historical and so on.... All studies grow out of relations in the one great common world. When the child lives in varied but concrete and active relationship to this common world, his studies are naturally unified."

Furthermore, children are not restricted to language only in which to explore, extend, and share their learning. Whole Language teachers invite their students to explore multiple meaning systems such as dance, art, photography, and music, recognizing that in our continual learning quest there are multiple paths to meaning. Language, in this sense, is expanded to encompass a range of visual and performing arts; Whole Language embraces alternative ways of creating and communicating the exploration of knowledge and imagination.

To understand the difference between a traditional approach in which students learn about language through isolated instructional activities and Whole Language, in which students learn about language incidentally as they use it to learn, let's step inside the Whole Language classroom of Betty Doerr, a fourth grade teacher at Fair Oaks School.

Fair Oaks, a Whole Language, bilingual school in Redwood City, California, a working class community fifteen miles south of San Francisco, is the poorest in the district. Ringed by dilapated apartment buildings on three sides and an industrial park on the other, the school is 86% Hispanic. Many students are recent arrivals from war-torn El Salvador and Nicaragua or economic refugees from Mexico. In 1987 a large housing project was built next to the school, bringing with it a thriving drug culture. As a result, when students arrive at school in the morning, they find used syringes on the playground and bullet holes in their classrooms. In August, 1990, an arson-set fire burned three classrooms to the ground; smoke, water damage, and exposed asbestos made three others unuseable. It was after the fire that Betty Doerr's fourth graders decided that they weren't going to take it any more; they were fed up, they wanted to reclaim their community from the drug dealers. But, as ten year olds, what impact could they have? What could they do to rid their community of drugs?

Doerr responded to their concerns by helping them to define their questions and plot their course of learning through a "theme cycle" (Edelsky, Altwerger, & Flores, 1991). First, gathering together on the rug at the front of the classroom, they brainstormed what they knew about the problem. The children were quick to identify and pool their knowledge: They knew where the dealers congregated and knew what buildings and streets to avoid; they were familiar with an array of drug and street language and had some idea of what drugs were available, who was selling, and who was buying.

Once they had defined what they knew about the problem, Doerr led them into the second part of the theme cycle: what they didn't know and what they wanted to find out. She asked them to brainstorm their questions and the children quickly responded:

- Why do people turn to drugs; what is so seductive about drugs?
- Why have drug dealers achieved such a stronghold in the Fair Oaks community; what is it about the community that enables drugs to flourish?
- What can they do as kids to combat the problem? Can they participate in the community group that is working to rid the area of drugs?
- Can they trust the police? (After all, many students are illegal immigrants, you hide when you see the police — you don't solicit their help.)
- Where does cocaine come from? What is it? Is there a way to prevent it from coming into this country?
- What is the government doing to stop the flow?

The students had indentified a list of questions. Next, as the third part of the theme cycle, Doerr asked them to think of ways in which they could find answers to their questions. What resources could they utilize in their search for answers? Again, the students brainstormed possible avenues they could explore for information:

- They agreed to read the daily newspaper and to bring in pertinent news clippings.

- They voted to watch, listen, and monitor news about the drug problem (community, state, and national) on television and radio.
- Reference books were identified as a probable source of information.
- The students realized that their best source of information might be people, both those who were involved in the drug culture and those who were fighting it, such as the sheriff, police, and community leaders.

The launching of the theme cycle was complete; the students had identified their existing knowledge base, the questions that remained, and resources they could utilize in their search for answers. What followed was two months of intensive research. They wrote letters to the sheriff, voicing their concerns about the drug culture that had invaded their school and community. He responded by coming to their classroom and participating in an intense discussion with the students. The Redwood City Police Department has since "adopted" Fair Oaks School; police officers visit the school regularly, chatting with students over lunch, tutoring them on a variety of subjects, and working to develop a positive relationship with students who, in the past, have had reason to be suspicious of them.

Doerr's students have also become involved in the community group organized to combat the drug problem. Rather than just taking the notes home to their parents about community meetings, the students are now participating themselves. They presented their perspective to the community group, explaining how the invasion of drugs was impacting them as kids, what it was like to come to school in the morning and find fresh bullet holes in their classroom blackboard. They also became involved in a study of the coca plant, learning how it is harvested and how crack and cocaine are manufactured. They learned about the coca trade and the variety of government measures designed to prevent the drugs from reaching this country. And, of course, throughout the inquiry process, the students wrote, read, and researched, interviewed experts on the topic, and presented their findings to each other and to community members. They were using language for real purposes and in the process they were learning what language is and what language can do.

This example illustrates one of the hallmarks of Whole Language: authenticity (Edelsky, 1984). It also reveals the holistic nature of Whole Language; that is, school and real life are not separated. Following the lead of John Dewey, Whole Language teachers believe that school *is* life and as such should not be conducted as a sterile preparation for living in the real world some day. Accordingly, students like Betty Doerr's fourth graders participate in "authentic" projects to answer the big questions and big ideas *they* have. Whole Language educators respect and honor their students as thoughtful, sensitive human beings, and they find ways to support their students' ideas and questions about social and physical phenomena. Eleanor Duckworth (1987) reminds us that it is in the having of such ideas that we find the essence of intellectual development. In this way, in-school living is as integrated and unified as out-of-school living; in fact, the two merge so that in thriving Whole Language classrooms the children's school and out-of-school lives are nearly seamless.

A Theory of Community

One may further note that the confrontation of the drug problem at Fair Oaks also illustrates how Whole Language creates community both inside and outside the school. As Ken Goodman has written (1991), "a Whole Language classroom is a democratic community of learners, and its curriculum is embedded in the culture and social experiences of the larger community." Whole Language educators begin to build a sense of community and democracy within their classrooms. Drawing on work of Paulo Freire (1970, 1973), they understand that it is not possible to rely on autocratic teaching methods to educate students as informed citizens who can participate in and contribute to a democratic society. Accordingly, students and teachers negotiate all aspects of the curriculum as well as the structure and daily routine that supports and nutures classroom life. They engage in constant reflection about what is working, what is not working, and they revise and change the structure and routine as needed.

This sense of community and democracy extends beyond the classroom as well. Whole Language educators like Betty Doerr work hard with parents and other community members to make their schools a viable part of the community in which they serve. Community members bring their experience into the schools to share with students; students step outside the bounds of their classrooms to interact with and learn from people outside the school. In this way, students develop an awareness of the issues facing their community, and, with the help of their teacher, they may begin to find ways to effect positive change.

Another example of community-based learning is the work of Eliot Wigginton (1986) with high school English students in Rabun Gap, Georgia. As a traditional high school teacher in the sixties, Wigginton responded to his students, dissatisfied with the traditional English high school curriculum of grammar drills, the five-part essay, and lectures on the symbolism of literature, by asking them what they were interested in and would like to study. After much discussion and negotiation, the students realized that they were living in a community rich in local history and folkcraft. Many of the local artisans and storytellers were quite elderly; once they died, their special abilities and knowledge would die with them. Students noted that they could both meet their curricular needs and serve their community by helping to perserve this history. The result became known as the Foxfire Project. Students gave up their English textbooks in favor of clipboards, tape recorders, and cameras and went out into their community to capture on tape, written notes, and photographs the ways of living represented by the local artisans and craftspeople. The students learned such skills and crafts as what to do with "barn sour pigs," how to read the weather, where to find medicinal plants and herbs and the best techniques for building a log cabin. Their audio tapes were transcribed, background information and photographs were added, and the essays and pictures were published as the "Foxfire" magazine, named after a local plant that grew in caves and under rocks and glowed in the dark. In 1972 Doubleday bought the rights to the magazine, bound the issues together, and published the first Foxfire book. Now, nearly twenty years later there are nine Foxfire books. Two million copies are in print; it is one of the most successful publishing ventures Doubleday has ever undertaken. And, as Wigginton enjoys noting, much of it has been written, edited, and published by high school students who "hate" English.

A Theory of Teaching

Just as Whole Language embraces and celebrates the whole child, so Whole Language teachers are respected and valued as skilled and knowledgeable professional educators. Since the twenties, American school teachers have functioned as little more than technicians, following the scripted lesson plans of textbooks and basals and implementing curriculum controlled by standardized tests or the packaged materials of commerical publishers (Goodman, Shannon, Freeman, & Murphy, 1988; Shannon, 1989, 1990). As Ken Goodman has stated (1991), Whole Language is a "coming of age as professionals" for teachers. Whole Language teachers are discovering the full professional range of a true educator: teaching as inquiry, curricular and instructional decision making, authentic assessment, and political involvement.

Teaching as inquiry is a hallmark of Whole Language (Watson, Burke, & Harste, 1989). Whole Language teachers throw off the shackles of textbooks and management systems; they reject the unauthentic assessment of standardized tests. Drawing on their understanding of language and learning, of curriculum and pedagogy, they engage in classroom inquiry, taking their instructional and curricular cues from their students. Learning experiences arise not from the pages of textbooks or programmed curriculum, but from the needs and interests of students as well as from the community of which the school is part.

Whole Language teachers conduct much of their classroom inquiry utilizing the strategies of authentic assessment. Unlike standardized tests and other traditional evaluative measures which are separate from the classroom curriculum and added on at the beginning or end of a semester, authentic assesment is a continuous process and an integral part of the curriculum. Teachers use a variety of data-gathering strategies that are not unlike the ethnographic tools of the anthropologist. These include anecdedotal records of classroom learning experiences and individual student response, holistic checklists, parent–teacher–student conferences and interviews, and student learning logs and portfolios. Teachers become researchers in their own classrooms, careful observers of their students as learners, and this way, they are able to make sensitive and informed decisions regarding student-centered instruction and curriculum. They also understand that the most important kind of evaluation is self-evalution. As self-awareness enables students to effectively monitor and control their own learning, teachers invite and encourage their students to participate in continual self-reflection; to step outside their learning experiences and from this more objective stance engage in self-analysis. Self-reflection is a critical component of professional life; accordingly, Whole Language educators engage in continuous self-evaluation themselves: What is working well in the classroom? What isn't working as well? How shall we revise our curriculum and instruction to better meet the needs and interests of our students?

The same decision making that characterizes Whole Language teachers inside their classrooms holds true outside the classroom as well. Whole Language teachers are involved in professional conferences, workshops, and courses, both as participants and presenters. As they reject the traditional educational system which has suppressed the creative spirit of teaching, Whole Language teachers have turned to each other for support and inspiration. Across the United States and Canada, teacher support groups, variously known under such acronyms as TAWL (Teachers Applying Whole Language), SMILE (Support and Maintenance for Implementing Language Experience) and CEL (Child-Centered, Experience-Based Learning), meet on a weekly or monthly basis to share triumphs and concerns. Often not finding the needed professional support at institutes for teacher education, many groups have taken a leading role in organizing professional development institutes and conferences for their colleagues.

In February, 1989, these separate teacher support groups banded together under one confederation, The Whole Language Umbrella. Three years since its founding, The Umbrella now represents more than one hundred groups, sponsors an annual conference, publishes a quarterly newsletter, and provides its members with a number of professional and political services, including a "hotline" that "educators under siege" can call for help and advice. In many communities across the country, Whole Language teachers have met the resistance of right wing groups, who want to preserve a narrow, restrictive approach to education. Through the hotline, these embattled teachers receive packets of articles carefully outlining the major tenets of Whole Language and answering some of the most frequently asked questions ("Why don't you teach phonics?"). They are also given the names of Whole Language educators and researchers in their area who have indicated a willingness to help. A political action committee within The Umbrella is aggressively working to strengthen the organization and better define needed steps to combat right wing influences and misunderstandings. For too long, teachers have been naive about the political nature of education and about their role as political ambassadors. Whole Language is striving to overcome this ignorance.

Education and Politics

More than 150 years ago, Jules Michelet (1846) asked, "What is the first part of politics? Education. The second? Education. And the third? Education." Two hundred years ago, Thomas Jefferson pointed out that an educated electorate is necessary for the survival of a democracy. The natural unification of politics and education in Whole Language is reflected in the shared power base between teachers and students as they negotiate how they will live together in their classrooms. Students are invited to voice their needs and interests regarding every aspect of curricular planning as well as classroom organization. What is more, Whole Language teachers agree with Paulo Freire (Freire & Macedo, 1987) that we must "read the world" as we read the word. Whole Language teachers reject not only the instructional control of the basal reading technology that has served to de-skill them as professionals, but also its shallow, narrow view of the purpose of reading. The basals may teach students how to decode words and reproduce the meaning of the author's text, but as Patrick Shannon (1989) argues, "we were promised much more." Echoing Freire he writes:

> Reading ... is supposed to enable us to read both the word and the world in ways that allow us to see through the mysteries, ambiguities, and deceit of modern living in order to make sense of our lives, to understand the connections among our lives and those of others, and to act on our new knowledge to construct a better, a more just, world. (p. viii)

Whole Language educators accept this challenge. They engage their students in deeply thoughtful and critical discussions regarding their experiences in the classroom and the world at large. And like Betty Doerr's fourth graders at Fair Oaks, students are encouraged to take action, to do what they can to make a positive difference.

Whole Language teachers are taking action against such harmful and inhumane educational practices and beliefs as ability grouping, tracking, retention, deficit myths surrounding ethnic and regional dialects, and standardized tests; all have traditionally served to disenfranchise specific minority populations. Whole Language teachers are assuming an increasingly political role as they refuse to adopt such practices in their own classrooms and work to convince their colleagues, administrators, and local, state, and national policy makers to do the same.

Pam Howard (1991) provides an example of a parent who decided to fight Arizona's policy regarding standardized testing. It was a decision she made after a visit to her son's first grade class while they were taking the Iowa Test of Basic Skills. Watching the children cry with frustration as they struggled with the ambiguous test questions, she was repelled by the whole process. She writes, "I knew that I had to voice my concerns about the effects of standardized testing on first-grade children." Joined by a group of Whole Language educators from Phoenix, Howard founded CESE (Community for Effective Student Evaluation) and together they lobbied the state legislature to change the law regarding the statewide testing of first, second, and twelfth graders. The group argued that testing primary age children was inhumane as these children lacked the abilities and experience to handle the strenuous testing regimen. They also maintained that testing twelfth graders was a waste of time and money since these students graduated before the results were known. Two years of lobbying resulted in the passage of a bill eliminating testing for first and twelfth graders. Howard writes that it was a long, frustrating struggle, but that every time she thought of giving up, she was reminded of the "crying six-year olds in my son's first grade class ... I knew I had to keep going."

Whole Language educators recognize that the liberating changes that they and their students experience through Whole Language will have no lasting impact unless they concern themselves with greater social change that will help all members of our society realize the promises of our democracy. As Michael Apple (1991) warns:

> For all its meritorious goals, the Whole Language movement cannot insure that its own goals and methods will have a lasting and widespread impact unless it is willing to act not only within the school, but outside it as well. Its proponents need to join with others in the wider social movements that aim at democratizing our economy, politics, and culture, and that act against a society that is so unequal in gender, race, and class terms.

Whole Language as both a movement and a philosophy is dynamic and evolving; today's beliefs and practices are extended and refined tomorrow as Whole Language educators conduct their own research or read the findings of others, and reflect on, evaluate, and revise their teaching art. Unlike limited educational fads that come and go with the marketing whims and strategies of educational publishers, Whole Language is not an instructional approach, a curricular program, or a new set of educational techniques. It is a profound philosophy, founded on humanistic traditions and scientific research, about who we are as human beings, how we learn, and how that process is best supported in classrooms. At its core is a belief in learning as the birthright of *every* human being: learning that is natural, life-affirming, and joyful.

References

Apple, M. (1991). Teachers, politics and whole language. In Kenneth S. Goodman, Lois Bridges Bird, & Yetta M. Goodman (Eds.), *The Whole Language Catalog*. New York: American School Publishers.

Atwell, N. (1987). *In the middle: Writing, reading and learning with adolescents.* Portsmouth, NH: Heinemann.

Bird, L. B. (1991). Whole language teachers do teach. In Kenneth S. Goodman, Lois Bridges Bird, & Yetta M. Goodman (Eds.), *The whole language catalog.* New York: American School Publishers.

Bird, L. B. (1987). What is whole language? In *Dialogue: Teachers Networking: The Whole Language Newsletter. 1*(1). New York: Owens.

Calkins, L. (1986). *The art of teaching writing.* Portsmouth, NH: Heinemann.

Calkins, L. (1991). *Living between the lines.* Portsmouth, NH: Heinemann.

Clay, M. (1975). *What did I write?* Portsmouth, NH: Heinemann.

Dewey, J. (1943). *The child and the curriculum and the school and the society.* New York: Collier.

Doake, D. (1981). *Book experience and emergent reading in preschool children.* Unpublished doctoral dissertation, University of Alberta, Canada.

Duckworth, E. (1987). The having of wonderful and other ideas and other essays on teaching and learning. New York: Teachers College Press.

Edelsky, C., Altwerger, B., & Flores B. (1991). *Whole language: What's the difference?* Portsmouth, NH: Heinemann.

Edelsky, C. (1990, Spring). Inservice for Fair Oaks School, Redwood City School District, Redwood City, CA.

Edelsky, C., & Smith, K. (1984). Is that writing or are those marks just a figment of your curriculum? *Language Arts 61*, 24–32.

Ferreiro, E., & Teberosky, A. (1982). *Literacy before schooling.* Portsmouth, NH: Heinemann.

Freire, P. (1970). *Pedagogy of the oppressed.* New York: Continuum.

Freire, P. (1973). *Education for critical consciousness.* New York: Continuum.

Freire, P., & Macedo, D. (1987). *Literacy: Reading the word and the world.* South Hadley, MA: Bergin & Garvey.

Goodman, K. S., & Goodman, Y. M. (1989). Introduction: Redefining education. In Lois Bridges Bird (Ed.), *Becoming a whole language school: The Fair Oaks Story.* Katonah, NY: Owens.

Goodman, K. S., & Goodman, Y. M. (1990). Vygotsky in a whole-language perspective. In Luis Moll (Ed.), *Vygotsky and education.* Cambridge, MA: Cambridge University Press.

Goodman, K. S. (1965). A linguistic study of cues and miscues in reading. *Elementary English Journal 42*, 39–44.

Goodman, K. S., Shannon, P., Freeman, Y. V., & Murphy, S. (1988). *Report card on basal readers*. Katonah, NY: Owen.

Goodman, Y. (1984). The development of initial literacy. In H. Goelman, A. Olberg, & F. Smith (Eds.), *Awakening to literacy*. Portsmouth, NH: Heinemann.

Graves, D. (1983). *Writing: Teachers and children at work*. Portsmouth, NH: Heinemann.

Graves, D., & Stuart, V. (1985). *Write from the start*. New York: Dutton.

Halliday, M. (1975). *Learning how to mean*. London: Arnold.

Halliday, M. (1978). Language as a social semiotic: The social interpretation of language and meaning. Baltimore: University Park Press.

Harste, J., Burke, C., & Woodward, V. (1984). *Language stories and literacy lessons*. Portsmouth, NH.: Heinemann.

Holdaway, D. (1979). *The foundations of literacy*. Portsmouth, NH: Heinemann.

Howard, P. (1991). One parent's fight against standardized testing. In Kenneth S. Goodman, Lois Bridges Bird, & Yetta M. Goodman (Eds.), *The whole language catalog*. New York: American School Publishers.

Kilpatrick, W. (1918). The project method. *Teachers College Record 19*, 318–334.

Miller, R. (1991). Pioneers. In Kenneth S. Goodman, Lois Bridges Bird, & Yetta M. Goodman (Eds.), *The whole language catalog*. New York: American School Publishers.

Newman, J. (1985). *Whole language: Theory in use*. Portsmouth, NH: Heinemann.

Piaget, J. (1952). *The origins of intelligence in children*. New York: Norton.

Shannon, P. (1989). *Broken promises: Reading instruction in twentieth-century America*. South Hadley, MA: Bergin & Garvey.

Shannon, P. (1990). *The struggle to continue: Progressive reading instruction in the United States*. Portsmouth, NH.: Heinemann.

Smith, F. (1986). *Insult to intelligence: The bureaucratic invasion of our classrooms*. New York: Arbor House.

Stephens, D. (1992). *Research on whole language: Support for a new curriculum*. Katonah, NY: Owen.

Teale, W., & Sulzby, E. (Eds.). (1986). *Emergent literacy: Writing and reading*. Norwood, NJ.

Vygotsky, L. S. (1978). *Mind in society*. Ed. by M. Cole, V. John-Steiner, S. Scribner, and E.Souberman. Cambridge, MA: Harvard University Press.

Watson, D., Burke C., & Harste, J. (1989). *Whole language: Inquiring voices*. New York: Scholastic.

Weaver, C. (1990). *Understanding whole language: From principles to practice*. Portsmouth, NH: Heinemann.

Wigginton, E. (1986). *Sometimes a shining moment*. New York: Anchor Press/Doubleday.

Related Readings

Bateson, G. (1972). *Steps to an Ecology of Mind*. New York: Ballantine.

Berman, M. (1981). *The Reenchantment of the World*. Ithaca, NY: Cornell University Press.

Bohm, D., & Peat, F.D. (1987). *Science, Order and Creativity*. Toronto: Bantam.

Bowers, C.A., & Flinders, D. (1990). *Responsive Teaching: An Ecological Approach to Classroom Patterns of Language, Culture and Thought*. New York: Teachers College Press.

Bowers, C.A. (1992). *Education, Cultural Myths and the Ecological Crisis: Toward Deep Changes*. Albany: SUNY Press.

Bowers, C.A. (1993). *Recovery of the Ecological Imperative in Education and Social Thought: Critical Essays 1977-1992*. New York: Teachers College Press.

Capra, F., & Steindl-Rast, D. (1991). *Belonging to the Universe*. San Francisco: Harper.

Edelsky, C. (1991). *With Literacy and Justice for All: Rethinking the Social in Language and Education*. New York: Falmer.

Gatto, J.T. (1992). *Dumbing Us Down: The Hidden Curriculum of Compulsory Schooling*. Philadelphia: New Society.

Gough, N. From Epistemology to Ecopolitics: Renewing a Paradigm for Curriculum. *Journal of Curriculum Studies*, 21(3), 225-241.

Johnston, P.H. (1992). *Constructive Evaluation of Literate Activity*. New York: Longman.

Lemkow, A. (1990). *The Wholeness Principle: Dynamics of Unity Within Science, Religion and Society*. Wheaton, IL: Quest.

Miller, J.P. (1988). *The Holistic Curriculum*. Toronto: OISE Press.

Miller, J.P., & Drake, S. (Eds.). (1992). *Holistic Education in Practice* (Theme issue of *Orbit*). Scarborough, Ontario: Nelson.

Miller, R. (1992). *What Are Schools For? Holistic Education in American Culture* (2nd ed.). Brandon, VT: Holistic Education Press.

Oliver, D., & Gershman, K. (1989). *Education, Modernity and Fractured Meaning*. Albany: SUNY Press.

Orr, D. (1992). *Ecological Literacy: Education and the Transition to a Postmodern World*. Albany: SUNY Press.

Palmer, P. (1983). *To Know As We Are Known: A Spirituality of Education*. San Francisco: Harper & Row.

Purpel, D. (1989). *The Moral & Spiritual Crisis in Education: A Curriculum for Justice & Compassion in Education*. Granby, MA: Bergin & Garvey.

Rifkin, J. (1991). *Biosphere Politics*. New York: Crown.

Roszak, T. (1978). *Person/Planet: The Creative Disintegration of Industrial Society*. Garden City, NY: Anchor/Doubleday.

Roszak, T. (1992). *The Voice of the Earth*. New York: Simon & Schuster.

Shannon, P. (1989). *Broken Promises: Reading Instruction in Twentieth Century America*. Westport, CT: Bergin & Garvey/Greenwood.

Shannon, P. (1990). *The Struggle to Continue: Progressive Reading Instruction in the United States*. Portsmouth, NH: Heinemann.

Sloan, D. (1983). *Insight-Imagination: The Recovery of Thought and the Modern World*. Westport, CT: Greenwood.

Sloan, D. (Ed.). (1984). *Toward the Recovery of Wholeness: Knowledge, Education and Human Values*. New York: Teachers College Press.

Willis, G., & Schubert, W.H. (1991). *Reflections from the Heart of Educational Inquiry: Understanding Curriculum and Teaching Through the Arts*. Albany: SUNY Press.

Contributors

Douglas Sloan is Professor of History and Education and Director of the Center for the Study of the Spiritual Foundations of Education at Teachers College, Columbia University. He is also Director of the Masters Program at the Waldorf Institute of Sunbridge College.

Ron Miller is an independent scholar whose primary interest is the social and historical context of alternative, progressive and holistic educational approaches. He was the founding publisher/editor of *Holistic Education Review* from 1988 through 1991, and established Holistic Education Press in 1990. He also helped to launch the Global Alliance for Transforming Education and was a principal author of its mission statement, *Education 2000: A Holistic Perspective*. Miller is the author of *What Are Schools For? Holistic Education in American Culture* (Holistic Education Press, 1990/1992) and he is currently writing a new book of essays, *Caring for New Life: Reflections on Education and Culture*. He is also working with colleagues to establish a center for educational studies in Burlington, Vermont.

David W. Orr is Professor of Environmental Studies at Oberlin College. Before going to Oberlin in 1990, he was the co-founder of the Meadowcreek Project, a 1500-acre environmental education center located in Fox, Arkansas. He is the author of *Ecological Literacy: Education and the Transition to a Postmodern World* (State University of New York Press, 1991), and co-editor with David Eagan of *The Campus and Environmental Responsibility* (Jossey-Bass, 1992). He has also written for *Bioscience, The Environmental Professional, Harvard Educational Review, Holistic Education Review, Conservation Biology, Ecological Economics, Annals of Earth*, and other journals. He is a trustee of the Jessie Smith Noyes Foundation, a member of the Pew Scholars Advisory Board, education editor for *Conservation Biology*, and a member of the *Orion* magazine advisory board.

C. A. Bowers teaches in the area of educational studies at Portland State University. In addition to presenting the John Dewey Memorial Lecture, he has written widely on themes relating to the cultural and educational nature of the ecological crisis. He has also written on the political and cultural characteristics of educational computing. His articles have appeared in a variety of journals, including *The Trumpeter* and *Environmental Ethics.* His most recent books include *Education, Cultural Myths, and the Ecological Crisis: Toward Deep Changes* (State University of New York Press) and *Recovery of the Ecological Imperative in Education and Social Thought: Critical Essays, 1977-1992* (Teachers College Press).

Jack Miller has worked in the area of humanistic/holistic education for approximately twenty years. He is currently Head of Niagara Centre and Professor in Curriculum at the Ontario Institute for Studies in Education, where he also coordinates a program in holistic education at the graduate level. Jack is author and co-author of several books including *The Compassionate Teacher, Curriculum: Perspectives and Practice,* and *The Holistic Curriculum.* He is co-author of a new book entitled *Holistic Learning: A Teacher's Guide to Integrated Studies* (OISE Press).

David Purpel received his bachelor's degree in History from Tufts College and doctorate from Harvard University. He has taught in the Newton (Mass.) public schools, at the Harvard Graduate School of Education, and at the University of North Carolina at Greensboro. His research and teaching has focused on teacher education, supervision, moral education, and curriculum theory. His most recent book is *The Moral and Spiritual Crisis in Education* and he has edited with Svi Shapiro a book titled *Critical Social Issues in Education: Toward the 21st Century* (Longmans, 1992).

Kathleen Kesson is a core faculty member at Goddard College in Vermont, where she is working to develop a graduate program in holistic education. At Oklahoma State University, where she did her doctoral work, she served as Research Associate for the Institute for the Study of Alternative Paradigms in Education and taught classes in pedagogy and the social foundations of education. Kathleen has authored numerous journal articles, serves on the Editorial Board of the *Holistic Education Review,* and is an active member of the American Educational Research Association. She is the recent winner of the annual Ted Aoki Award in the field of curriculum.

Jeffrey Kane is Dean of Adelphi University's School of Education. He received his doctoral degree from New York University in the Philosophy of Science and is the author of *Beyond Empiricism: Michael Polanyi Reconsidered* (Peter Lang, 1984). His interest in epistemological issues extends to the study of the relationship between the development of human intelligence through the formal means of schooling and the nature and responsibility of government in a democratic society — the subject of his monograph, "In Fear of Freedom: Public Education and Democracy in America" (Myrin Institute for Adult Education, 1984). He has authored numerous journal articles and is currently editor of *Holistic Education Review*.

Lois Bridges Bird works as a whole language consultant with educators across the country, teaches at San Jose State University, and is the author/editor of three books: *Becoming a Whole Language School: The Fair Oaks Story* (Richard C. Owen, 1989), and with Ken and Yetta Goodman, *The Whole Language Catalog* (American School Publishers, 1991) and *The Whole Language Catalog Supplement on Authentic Assessment* (American School Publishers, 1992).